CADOGAN CHESS BOOKS

£3.95

The New
Bogo-Indian

CADOGAN CHESS SERIES

Chief Advisor: Garry Kasparov
Editor: Andrew Kinsman
Russian Series Editor: Ken Neat

Other opening titles from Cadogan include:

VLADIMIR BAGIROV
English Opening: Classical and Indian
English Opening: Symmetrical

MICHAEL BASMAN
The Killer Grob
The New St George

JOHN DONALDSON and JEREMY SILMAN
Accelerated Dragons

SVETOZAR GLIGORIC
Nimzo-Indian Defence

DAVID NORWOOD
The Modern Benoni

LYEV POLUGAYEVSKY
The Sicilian Labyrinth (Volumes 1 & 2)

EGON VARNUSZ
Play Anti-Indian Systems
Play the Caro-Kann

JOHN WATSON
Play the French

For a complete catalogue of CADOGAN CHESS books (which includes the Pergamon Chess and Maxwell Macmillan Chess lists) please write to:
Cadogan Books plc, London House, Parkgate Road, London SW11 4NQ
Tel: (071) 738 1961 Fax: (071) 924 5491

The New Bogo-Indian

Shaun Taulbut

CADOGAN CHESS
LONDON, NEW YORK

CADOGAN BOOKS DISTRIBUTION

UK/EUROPE/AUSTRALASIA/ASIA/AFRICA
Distribution: Grantham Book Services Ltd, Isaac Newton Way, Alma Park Industrial Estate, Grantham, Lincs NG31 9SD
Tel: (0476) 67421 Fax: (0476) 590223

USA/CANADA/LATIN AMERICA/JAPAN
Distribution: Paramount Distribution Center, Front and Brown Streets, Riverside, New Jersey 08075, USA
Tel: (609) 461 6500 Fax: (609) 764 9122

First published 1985 as *Play the Bogo-Indian* by Pergamon Press
This revised edition published 1994 by Cadogan Books plc, London House, Parkgate Road, London SW11 4NQ

Copyright © 1985, 1994 Shaun Taulbut

British Library Cataloguing in Publication Data
A CIP catalogue record for this book is available from the British Library.

ISBN 1 85744 026 9

Typesetting by B. B. Enterprises
Printed in Great Britain by BPC Wheatons Ltd, Exeter

Contents

Bibliography

Books

Clarke, P.H., *Petrosian's Best Games of Chess* (G. Bell & Sons 1964)
Hooper, D. & Whyld, K., *Oxford Companion to Chess*, second edition (Oxford University Press 1992)
Kmoch, H., *Rubinstein's Chess Masterpieces* (Dover 1960)
Levy, D. & O'Connell, K., *Oxford Encyclopedia of Chess Games* (Oxford University Press 1981)
Smyslov, V., *Smyslov's 125 Selected Games* (Pergamon 1983, Cadogan 1994)

Periodicals

British Chess Magazine
Chess
Informator

Electronic

ChessBase

Historical Introduction

The basic starting position of the Bogo-Indian Defence arises after the opening sequence

1	d4	♘f6
2	c4	e6
3	♘f3	♗b4+

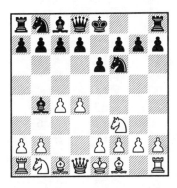

Black's third move is quite straightforward: the king's bishop is developed and castling is now prepared. However, as we shall see, there are a great deal of interesting possibilities for both sides from this position.

The originator of this opening is not known, but it has become known as the Bogo-Indian after Efim Bogolyubov, one of the leading players in the world in the 1920s and 1930s. A Ukrainian by birth, he became a German citizen following internment in Germany during the 1914-1918 war. His major tournament successes were as follows:

Pistyan 1922 1st ahead of Alekhine
Carlsbad 1923 1st with Alekhine and Maroczy
Breslau 1925 1st ahead of Rubinstein and Nimzowitsch
Moscow 1925 1st ahead of Lasker and Capablanca
Bad Kissingen 1928 1st ahead of Capablanca, Euwe, Rubinstein and Nimzowitsch.

Bogolyubov twice challenged Alekhine for the world championship (in 1929 and 1934) but was outclassed and lost both matches. He played the Bogo-Indian in his match with Rubinstein in 1920 (given below), but it had already had a number of outings before then. It was first tried out (in slightly different form) by the strong English player Buckle in his match against Löwenthal at London 1851.

Game 1
Löwenthal-Buckle
London (4th match game) 1851

1	d4	e6		11	♖b1	♖e8
2	c4	♗b4+		12	c5	

Buckle may have thought of this idea following his win as White against Elijah Williams at London 1849, which opened with the moves 1 d4 e6 2 c4 f5 3 ♘f3 ♗b4+.

3	♘c3	♗xc3+
4	bxc3	f5
5	e3	♘c6

This is playable since the knight can be redeployed to good effect on e7 or a5.

6	♘f3	♘f6
7	♗d3	b6
8	0-0	♗b7

9	h3	0-0
10	♗a3	

This is not a good place for the bishop. White should fight to gain control of the e4 square with ♘d2 and f2-f3.

10	...	♘e7

White eliminates his doubled pawn, but Black has good prospects on the kingside and in the centre.

12	...	♘g6
13	♕e2	♘e4

Black takes advantage of his control of the central light squares.

14	♗xe4	♗xe4
15	♖b3	♕f6
16	♘d2	♗d5
17	c4	♗b7
18	♗b2	♕g5
19	f4	♕e7
20	♕f2	♗c6
21	♗a3	d6
22	cxd6	cxd6
23	♘f3	♕c7
24	♖c1	♕d7
25	♖bc3	♖ac8
26	♘d2	♗b7
27	♘f3	♖c7
28	♘d2	♖ec8
29	♗b2	♘e7
30	♔h2	b5

Black exchanges the white c-pawn in order to be able to gain control of the d5 square.

31	cxb5	♖xc3
32	♗xc3	♘d5
33	♗b2	♖xc1
34	♗xc1	♕xb5

Black now has superior piece activity and White has a number of weaknesses to defend.

35	♘f3	♘c3
36	♘g5	♕d5
37	a3	h6
38	♘f3	a5
39	♕c2	♘e4
40	h4	

White prevents Black from expanding on the kingside with ...g7-g5.

40	...	♗c6
41	♗d2	a4
42	♗b4	♘f6
43	♗d2	♕b5
44	♗c1	♗xf3

Black exchanges his bishop to further wreck White's position.

| 45 | gxf3 | ♕f1 |

Now White cannot avoid losing material.

| 46 | d5 | |

46 ♕c8+ ♔h7 does not help White.

| 46 | ... | ♕xf3 |
| 47 | dxe6 | ♘e4 |

With the deadly threat of 48...♕g3+.

48	♕g2	♕h5
49	♔h3	g5
50	fxg5	hxg5
51	♔h2	g4
52	♕c2	♕xh4+
53	♔g2	♕g3+
54	♔f1	♕f3+
55	♔e1	♕h1+
56	♔e2	♕g2+
57	♔d3	♕xc2+
58	♔xc2	g3

0-1

The Bogo-Indian (as we now know it) was also tried by the Hungarian Joseph Noa (who also experimented with its close colleagues, the Nimzo-Indian and the Queen's Indian) in the 1880s.

Game 2
Mackenzie-Noa
London 1883

1	♘f3	e6
2	d4	♘f6
3	c4	♗b4+
4	♗d2	♗xd2+
5	♘bxd2	0-0
6	e3	♘c6

Black should establish his central pawns on the dark squares with ...d7-d6 and ...e6-e5, but this method of play did not become established until its adoption by Lasker in the 1920s. With 6...♘c6 Black transposes to a

Queen's Gambit Declined where he cannot attack White's centre with ...c7-c5.

7	♗d3	d5
8	♖c1	♗d7
9	0-0	♕e7
10	♗b1	♖ac8
11	a3	e5
12	cxd5	♘xd5
13	♕b3	♘b6
14	dxe5	♘xe5
15	♘xe5	♕xe5
16	♘f3	♕e7
17	♕d3	g6

Black is forced to weaken his kingside pawn constellation and this is the cause of his downfall.

18	♕c3	♖fe8
19	h3	♗c6
20	♘d4	♗d5
21	♖fe1	c5
22	♘e2	♘d7
23	♘g3	♕g5
24	e4	♗c6
25	♖e3	b6?

A bad mistake, overlooking White's obvious threat. 25...♖cd8 was better, to meet 26 ♘f5 with 26...♕f6 when there is no fork on d6 if the queens are exchanged.

26	♘f5	♖e5
27	h4	♕f6
28	♘h6+	♔f8
29	♘g4	♕e6
30	♘xe5	♘xe5
31	♗a2	♕d6
32	♗d5	♖e8
33	♗xc6	♕xc6
34	♖d1	♔g8
35	♖d5	♘g4 *(D)*
36	♖ed3	♕c7
37	g3	♘e5

White has won the exchange and is able to win comfortably by exchanging pieces.

38	♖d1	♘c6
39	♕c4	♕c8
40	♔g2	♘d4
41	f3	h5
42	b4	♘e6
43	bxc5	♘xc5
44	♖d6	♔g7
45	♕d4+	♔h7
46	♕f6	♖g8
47	♕xf7+	♖g7
48	♕f6	♕a6
49	♕b2	♕b7
50	♖1d5	♕e7
51	♕d4	♖f7
52	♖e5	1-0

An early setback for the new opening, but Black's strategy in this game has little in common with modern methods.

Until Bogolyubov tried it out in match against Rubinstein in 1920, the new opening had received little attention, but from then on Black players began to develop a more sophisticated way of handling it.

Game 3
Rubinstein-Bogolyubov
Sweden (Game 10) 1920

1	d4	♘f6
2	c4	e6
3	♘f3	♗b4+
4	♗d2	♗xd2+
5	♕xd2	b6

This leads to a Queen's Indian type position in which White has better control of the centre.

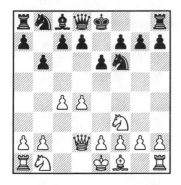

6	♘c3	♗b7
7	g3	

A later game between Sämisch and Spielmann (Moscow 1925) continued instead with 7 ♕c2, when Black decided to disrupt White's play with the exchange 7...♗xf3 8 gxf3 ♘c6 9 e3 ♕e7 10 f4 0-0 11 a3 ♘d8 12 ♗g2 c6 13 0-0 d5 14 cxd5 cxd5 15 ♖ac1 ♘b7 16 f5 ♘d6 17 fxe6 fxe6 18 f4 ♘g4 19 ♕e2 ♕h4 20 ♗f3 h5 21 ♖c2 ♘f5 22 ♗xg4 hxg4 23 ♕e1 ♕h3 24 ♘d1 ♖f6 25 ♖g2 ♖g6 26 ♔h1 ♖c8 27 ♘f2 ♕xe3 28 ♘xg4 ♕xe1 29 ♖xe1 ♘xd4

30 h4 ♘f3 0-1. Black should consider a similar strategy to this, since in the text game White obtained a firm grip on the centre.

7	...	0-0
8	♗g2	d6
9	0-0	♘bd7
10	♕c2	♖e8
11	e4	e5
12	♖ad1	exd4
13	♘xd4	♘c5
14	♖fe1	

White has the initiative since he can aim to dislodge the black knight on c5 with b2-b4 and can also play for a central advance with f2-f4 and e4-e5.

14	...	a5
15	f4	♕c8
16	h3	♘fd7
17	♔h2	♘b8

Black's pieces present an ugly picture, but he has no obvious weaknesses and it is difficult for

White to break through.

18	♘f5	g6
19	♘h6+	♔g7
20	♘g4	h5
21	♘e3	♘bd7
22	♘ed5	♗xd5
23	cxd5	

White has a strong position in the centre and Black has a weak pawn on c7, so Black must generate counterplay quickly before he is squashed. Bogolyubov does this admirably by probing the dark squares on the kingside.

23	...	h4
24	g4	

If White exchanges with 24 gxh4 then Black obtains counterplay with ...♕d8 and ...♖h8.

24	...	g5

A fine positional sacrifice; if White captures on g5 then Black obtains a superb outpost for his knight on e5.

25	e5	gxf4
26	e6	

26	...	♘e5
27	♕f5	fxe6
28	dxe6	♕xe6

Black offers the sacrifice of the exchange since after 28...♖b8 29 ♖xe5 gives White a strong attack. Now if 29 ♗xa8 ♕xf5 30 gxf5 ♖xa8 and Black has very good compensation for the exchange, so Rubinstein elects to capture the pawn on f4.

29	♕xf4	♖ac8
30	♕g5+	♕g6
31	♕xh4	♖e6
32	♕g3	c6
33	♖f1	♖f8
34	♖xf8	♔xf8
35	♘e2	♖f6
36	♘f4	♕g5
37	♘h5	♖g6
38	♖f1+	♔e7
39	♕f2	♕h6
40	♕d4	♔d7
41	b4	axb4
42	♕xb4	♔c7
43	♖b1	♘cd7
44	♘g3	♕h8
45	♘f5	d5
46	♖e1	♘c5
47	♔g1	♖e6
48	♘d4	♖e8
49	♖f1	♘ed3
50	♕c3	♕e5
51	♖f7+	♖e7
52	♖xe7+	♕xe7 (D)

This endgame is finely balanced: Black has attacking chances against the white king, whereas White has a strong passed g-pawn.

53	♘f5	♕e2
54	♕d4	♕xa2
55	g5	♕c4
56	♕f6	♕f4
57	♕e7+	♘d7

64	♗h3	b3
65	h5	♘c5
66	♘e6+	♘xe6
67	♗xe6	♔d6
68	♗f5	♔e7
69	g6	♔f6
70	♔f4	c5
71	g7	♘d3+
72	♔e3	♔xg7
73	♔xd3	♔h6
	½-½	

58	♘g7	♕d4+
59	♔h1	♕a1+
60	♔h2	♕e5+
61	♕xe5+	♘3xe5
62	h4	b5
63	♔g3	b4

This fighting struggle brought the opening into focus and soon afterwards Emanuel Lasker devised the strategy of placing the black central pawns on dark squares, after exchanging the dark-squared bishops.

Game 4
Pokorny-Lasker
Maehrisch-Ostrau 1923

1	d4	♘f6
2	♘f3	e6
3	c4	♗b4+
4	♗d2	♗xd2+
5	♘bxd2	0-0
6	e4	d6
7	♕c2	♘c6
8	♖d1	♕e7
9	♗e2	e5

Black can now develop his bishop to g4, so White chooses to close the centre to defend d4.

10	d5	♘d8
11	h3	♘h5
12	♘g1	♘f4
13	♗f3	f5
14	♘e2	fxe4

15	♘xe4	♘g6
16	♗g4	♘f7
17	♗xc8	♖axc8
18	0-0	♘g5

19	♘xg5	♕xg5

Black now has attacking possibilities down the half open f-file. Although White has control of the e4 square, it is difficult to make use of this due to Black's pressure on the kingside.

20	♖d3	♕e7
21	♖g3	♖f7
22	♖g4	c6
23	♕e4	cxd5
24	cxd5	♖c5
25	b4	♖c7
26	♖c1	♖xc1+
27	♘xc1	♕c7
28	♘e2	♕c8

This subtle move threatens to take control of the c-file with ...♖c7 while keeping an eye on the kingside. White decides to jettison the f-pawn to obtain counterplay on the queenside, but it is not enough.

29	♔h2	♖xf2
30	♕e3	♕f8
31	♔g3	♖f1
32	♕xa7	♘e7
33	♕xb7	♖e1
34	♕b5	♘f5+
35	♔h2	♘e3
36	♘g3	♘xg4+
37	hxg4	♕d8
38	♔h3	♖e3
39	a4	g6
40	a5	♕g5
41	♕e8+	♔g7
42	♕d7+	♔h6
43	♕xd6	♕f4
44	g5+	♔xg5
45	♕e7+	♔h6
46	♕h4+	♕xh4+
47	♔xh4	♖b3
	0-1	

White must resign since all his pawns are captured by the energetic black rook.

After this game the Bogo-Indian began to blossom; it was employed several times at the important tournaments at Breslau 1925, Baden-Baden 1925 and Semmering 1926.

Game 5
Grünfeld-Bogulyubov
Breslau 1925

1	d4	♘f6
2	c4	e6
3	♘f3	♗b4+

4	♘bd2	

This move, retaining the tension in the centre, was an innovation at the time.

| 4 | ... | 0-0 |
| 5 | a3 | ♗e7 |

Also perfectly playable would have been an exchange of the bishop on d2 followed by a fianchetto of the queen's bishop with ...b7-b6.

6   e3

White could have seized the centre with 6 e4, as Black has declined to stake a claim in the centre. However, after 6...d5 7 e5 ♘fd7 8 exd5 cxd5 9 ♗d3 c5 a dynamic position is reached in which Black has only slightly the worse of it (see Chapter 4).

| 6 | ... | d5 |
| 7 | ♗d3 | ♘bd7 |

Black could also have tried 7...c5 8 dxc5 a5 with a perfectly playable game, or 7...b6, which is considered in Chapter 5.

8   0-0

More to the point is 8 b4.

| 8 | ... | c5 |

Black has a good position, since White cannot develop his queen's bishop easily and his op-

ponent therefore has time to complete his development.

9	♕e2	cxd4
10	exd4	b6
11	cxd5	♘xd5
12	♘c4	♗b7

A typical isolated queen's pawn position has arisen, though Black is well placed here since he has complete control of the d5 square. White still cannot develop his queen's bishop to an active square.

13	♗d2	♖c8
14	♘ce5	♗f6
15	♕e4	g6
16	♕g4	♘e7
17	♗e4	♗a6

The pressure mounts on the white position, so Grünfeld sacrifices the exchange in order to mount an attack on the kingside; but Bogolyubov defends coolly.

| 18 | ♕f4 | ♗xe5 |
| 19 | dxe5 | f5 |

White was threatening 20 ♕h6 followed by 21 ♘g5, so Black must defend by making room for his knight on f8.

| 20 | ♕h6 | ♖e8 |

Now if 21 ♘g5 ♘f8 defends adequately.

21	♗g5	fxe4
22	♗f6	♘f5
23	♕g5	♘xf6
24	exf6	0-1

Richard Réti, who had already played the opening against Vidmar at Mannheim 1914, used a plan similar to Lasker's in the following game.

Game 6
Michel-Réti
Semmering 1926

1	d4	♘f6
2	c4	e6
3	♘f3	♗b4+
4	♗d2	♗xd2+
5	♘bxd2	d6
6	e4	♛e7
7	♗d3	e5
8	0-0	0-0

9	♛c2	♘c6
10	♛c3	exd4

Here 10...♗g4 was also worthy of consideration.

11	♘xd4	♘xd4
12	♛xd4	♛e5
13	♘f3	

Instead 13 ♛xe5 dxe5 14 ♘f3 ♖e8 15 ♖fd1 ♗g4 gives Black an edge because of his potential control of the d4 square.

13	...	♛xd4
14	♘xd4	♖e8
15	♘b5	♖e7
16	♘c3	♗e6
17	f3	♘d7

18	♘d5	♗xd5
19	cxd5	♘c5
20	♗c2	a5

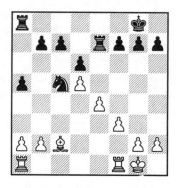

White must dislodge the black knight in order to make progress.

21	b3	♖ae8
22	a3	f5
23	b4	

After 23 exf5 ♖e2 24 ♖ac1 ♖d2 Black has good counterplay.

23	...	axb4
24	axb4	♘a6
25	♖fb1	fxe4
26	♗xe4	♖e5
27	♖b2	g6
28	♔f2	♔g7
29	♖a5	♔f6
30	♗d3	♖8e7
31	♖b5	

Much better was 31 ♗xa6 bxa6 32 ♖d2 when White can aim to capture the a6 pawn. Now the black knight is able to redeploy itself and Black takes control.

31	...	b6
32	♖a2	♘b8
33	♖a7	♖e3
34	♗e4	♖c3
35	♔e2	♖c2+
36	♔f1	♖c4
37	♔e2	♘d7
38	♔d2	♘e5
39	♗b1	♖d4+
40	♔c2	♖h4
41	h3	♘c4

42	♔c3	♘e3
43	g4	♖xh3
	0-1	

Not wishing to be outdone, Nimzowitsch adopted the line, developing a system based upon the move 4...♕e7 in response to 4 ♗d2 rather than exchanging the bishops with 4...♗xd2+.

Game 7
Fairhurst-Nimzowitsch
London 1927

1	d4	e6
2	c4	♘f6
3	♘f3	♗b4+
4	♗d2	♕e7
5	g3	♗xd2+
6	♘bxd2	d6
7	♗g2	0-0
8	0-0	h6
9	♕c2	♖e8
10	e4	e5
11	d5	a5
12	a3	

White should play more slowly with 12 b3 followed by 13 a3 since now Black is able to impede White's queenside play.

| 12 | ... | a4 |

Black is planning to position his knight on c5 where it will further restrain the white queenside.

13	c5	dxc5
14	♘c4	♘fd7
15	♖ad1	b5
16	d6	

This causes Black some temporary discomfort, but Black is able to retain his extra pawn.

16	...	♕e6
17	dxc7	♕xc4
18	cxb8(♕)	♖xb8
19	♕xc4	bxc4
20	♖d5	♖xb2
21	♖c1	f6

Defending the e-pawn allows the black knight to move to b6.

| 22 | ♗f1 | ♘b6 |

23	♖xc5	♗e6
24	♖c6	♗f7
25	♘d2	♖xd2
26	♖xb6	♖ed8

White cannot capture on c4 because of ...♖d1+.

27	♖b4	♖a2
28	♖b7	

28 ♗xc4 ♗xc4 29 ♖bxc4 ♖d2 30 ♖f1 ♖xa3 retains the advantage for Black.

28	...	♖c8
29	♖d1	c3
30	♖dd7	♗b3
31	♖xg7+	♔f8
32	♖g6	♖c6

33	♖xh6	♖b2
34	♖a7	♗g8
35	♖h8	c2
36	♖a8+	♔e7
37	♖a7+	♔d6
38	♖xg8	c1(♕)
39	♖d8+	♔c5
40	♖dd7	♕e1

0-1

Nimzowitsch also used the opening with success at New York 1927 (see the next chapter), and it became a useful weapon in the armoury of many of the strongest players.

Game 8
Marshall-Capablanca
Berlin 1928

1	d4	♘f6
2	♘f3	e6
3	c4	♗b4+
4	♗d2	♕e7
5	♘c3	

As Nimzowitsch showed in his game against Vidmar, Black can fianchetto his queen's bishop with the aim of controlling the central light squares.

5	...	b6
6	e3	♗xc3
7	♗xc3	♘e4
8	♖c1	♗b7
9	♗d3	0-0
10	0-0	d6
11	♘d2	♘xc3
12	♖xc3	c5

Black prefers this thrust to 12...e5 13 d5 when White has

possibilities on both sides of the board.

| 13 | dxc5 | dxc5 |

Marshall exchanges pawns in the centre in order to pursue a kingside attack, but this leaves his pieces rather awkwardly bunched on the d-file.

14	♕h5	h6
15	f4	♘d7
16	e4	e5

This blocks the white pawn on e4, which in turn stops the white bishop from attacking the kingside.

| 17 | ♘f3 | ♖ae8 |

Black reinforces his strongpoint on e5 and threatens to exchange on f4.

18	♘h4	exf4
19	♖xf4	♕g5

20	♕f3	♘e5
21	♕f2	♘xd3
22	♖xd3	♖xe4
23	♖xe4	♗xe4

24	♖e3	f5
25	h3	♖d8
26	a3	♖d1+
27	♔h2	♕f6
28	♕f4	g5
29	♖g3	♔f8
30	♕b8+	♖d8
31	♕e5	♕xe5
32	♘g6+	♔f7
33	♘xe5+	♔f6

0-1

White resigned since 34 ♘f3 f4 entombs the white rook.

In the 1930s Paul Keres started playing the opening, often with the sequence 1 d4 e6 2 c4 ♗b4+ (see Chapter 11 for a full discussion of the independent significance of this move order). Keres was one of the strongest players in the world for over 30 years and was very unlucky not to have an opportunity to play a match for the world championship. One of his most outstanding results was equal first at the 1938 AVRO tournament with Fine ahead of Capablanca, Alekhine, and Botvinnik. This game was played in the previous year.

Game 9
Trifunovic-Keres
Prague 1937

1	d4	e6
2	♘f3	♘f6
3	c4	♗b4+
4	♗d2	♕e7
5	g3	♘c6

A peculiar move at first sight, but its motivation will soon become clear. Black will have to exchange on d2 at some point in order not to lose time or get his bishop trapped when White moves his queen's bishop after castling, after which White has a choice of two main recaptures: ♕xd2 and ♘bxd2. The ideal set-up is for White to recapture on d2 with the queen and then play his queen's knight to c3 with the aim of playing e4, and 5...♗xd2+ 6 ♕xd2 ♘e4 7 ♕c2 ♕b4+ 8 ♘bd2 is satisfactory for White.

6 ♗g2 ♗xd2+

Why is it appropriate to exchange now? The point is that after 7 ♕xd2 ♘e4 8 ♕c2 ♕b4+ White must either play 9 ♘c3 ♘xc3 10 ♕xc3 ♕xc3+ 11 bxc3 with a good game for Black, because of the weakness of the white doubled pawns, or sacrifice a pawn with 9 ♘bd2 ♘xd2 10 ♕xd2 ♕xc4 when it is not clear that White has sufficient compensation.

7 ♘bxd2 d6

Black prepares to gain a central foothold with ...e6-e5.

8 ♘f1 0-0

9 ♘e3

White has manoeuvred his knight to e3 in order to counter Black's central ...e6-e5 thrust: after 9...e5 10 ♘d5 ♘xd5 11 cxd5 ♘xd4 12 ♘xd4 exd4 13 ♕xd4 White can put pressure on Black down the half-open c-file. Keres therefore switches his plan.

9 ... ♘e4

10 d5 ♘d8

Black refrains from opening the c-file by exchanging on d5.

11 ♘d4 ♘c5

12 b4 ♘a6

13 a3 e5

14 ♘df5 ♕f6

15 ♗e4 h5

Black hopes to drive back the knight on f5 by ...g7-g6, but Trifunovic has other ideas.

16 g4 g6

17 ♕d2

White sacrifices a piece to expose the black king but the monarch hurries away to a safe home.

17 ... gxf5

18 gxf5 ♖e8

19 h4 ♔f8

20 0-0-0 ♔e7

Black is a piece up, but can scarcely move any of his men. Meanwhile White can create an attack on the kingside.

21	♖dg1	♖h8
22	♖g5	♘b8
23	♘f1	a5
24	♘g3	axb4
25	♘xh5	♖xh5
26	♖xh5	

White has won back the exchange and now Black must defend against the threat of 27 ♖h6 followed by f5-f6+.

26	...	♘d7
27	♖h6	♘c5
28	♗c2	♕xf5

Black sacrifices a piece to activate his army; if he moves the queen, f5-f6+ is decisive.

29	♗xf5	♘b3+
30	♔c2	♘xd2
31	♗xc8	♘xc4
32	♗f5	♖xa3

The smoke has cleared and White has won the exchange for two pawns, and has a potential winner in his passed h-pawn. Surprisingly though, White is struggling, for his rook on h6 is ineffective, blocking the h-pawn, and the small black army on the queenside is highly dangerous.

33	♖h3	b5
34	♖b3	c5

The black infantry begins to roll. Obviously bad is 35 dxc6 ♘xc6 and the black knight is threatening to come to d4 with effect.

35	♖h8	e4

Black moves this pawn to e4 in order to block the diagonal of the bishop to b1 and to eliminate the d-pawn, so that the sleepy knight on d8 will be able to emerge. White cannot capture on e4, since Black captures on b3 and then wins with a knight fork.

36	h5	♖a2+
37	♔d1	♖d2+
38	♔e1	♖xd5
39	♗xe4	♖e5
40	♗b1	♘e6
41	e3	♘f8

Now the white rook on h8 cannot move for fear of losing the h-pawn.

42	♔e2	♖g5
43	♗e4	♖g4
44	♗f5	♖h4
45	♖b1	♘a3

Now if White remains passive with ♖b2, Black can play ...♔f6 (as in the game) with an exchange of knight for bishop, and then move his king to the queenside.

46	♖g1	b3
47	♖gg8	♔f6
48	♖xf8	♔xf5
49	♖xf7+	♔e6
50	♖a7	b2
51	♖h6+	♔d5
52	♖xa3	b1(♕)
53	♖d3+	♔c4
54	♖dxd6	♖h1
	0-1	

A superb struggle in which Keres revelled in the tactical complications.

The Bogo-Indian can also be used as a positional weapon, as demonstrated by Tigran Petrosian. This game demonstrates one of his ideas that remains popular today.

Game 10
Kalantar-Petrosian
Erevan 1948

1	d4	♘f6
2	c4	e6
3	♘f3	♗b4+
4	♗d2	♕e7
5	g3	♘c6
6	♗g2	♗xd2+
7	♘bxd2	0-0
8	0-0	d6
9	e4	a5

9...e5 seems more natural but the text is not bad. In this variation the centre is often closed, when White's main weapon is an advance with b2-b4 and c4-c5, so

9...a5 is a useful pre-emptive move.

10	♕c2

10 e5 is a critical test of this line - see Chapter 9.

10	...	♘d7
11	d5	♘cb8

If you were unaware that Petrosian was a very strong player, you might he surprised by his moves. However, his style was to tempt his opponents to overreach themselves, creating vulnerable points in their own camp that he could later exploit.

12	♘d4	♘c5
13	♕c3	e5
14	♘4b3	

14 ♘f5 ♗xf5 15 exf5 would be better for Black because of the weakness in White's pawn structure.

14	...	b6
15	♘xc5	bxc5

White has not achieved anything on the queenside. Black can use the half-open b-file to probe White's position, while White's bishop on g2 is hampered by his own centre pawns.

16	f4	♘d7

17	♗h3	♖e8
18	♖ae1	♕f6
19	♗xd7	♗xd7
20	fxe5	♕xe5
21	♕xe5	♖xe5
22	♘f3	♖e7
23	e5	

White has finally broken Black's grip on the central dark squares, but he is later forced to exchange pawns, leaving Black with an easy game.

23	...	♖ae8
24	exd6	♖xe1
25	♖xe1	♖xe1+
26	♘xe1	cxd6

This endgame favours Black, since his kingside majority can yield a passed pawn, while White's pawn majority on the queenside is permanently crippled. Black can also attempt to invade the white position with his king via e5 and d4, and the black bishop can threaten the white pawns which are fixed on the light squares.

27	♔f2	f5
28	♔e3	♔f7

29	♘d3	♗c8
30	b3	

White would have been forced to play this after Black plays ...♗a6. Now White must take great care not to let the bishop in, else all his pawns will be devoured.

30	...	g5
31	♔f3	♔f6
32	♔e3	♗d7
33	♔f3	♗e8
34	♔e3	h6
35	♔f3	

White cannot counterattack with his knight on the queenside: 35 ♘b2 ♗h5 36 ♘a4 ♔e5 37 ♘b6 f4+ 38 gxf4+ gxf4+ 39 ♔f2 ♗g4 and White is helpless to stop the black king marching to the queenside.

35	...	♗h5+
36	♔e3	♗d1
37	♔d2	♗f3
38	♔e3	♗e4

. Black is now winning, since moving the knight allows the black king to come to e5, e.g. 39 ♘c1 ♔e5 40 ♘e2 ♗b1 41 ♘c3 f4+ 42 ♔f2 ♗d3 and wins.

39	♔d2	♗xd3
40	♔xd3	♔e5

The rest is easy: Black can force a passed pawn whereas White cannot.

41	♔e3	f4+
42	gxf4+	gxf4+
43	♔f3	♔f5
44	♔f2	♔e4
45	♔e2	f3+
46	♔f2	♔f4
47	h4	h5
48	a3	♔e4
	0-1	

White is paralysed: 49 b4 axb4 50 axb4 cxb4 51 c5 ♔xd5 wins for Black.

Another world champion devotee of the Bogo is Vasily Smyslov. Here is a fine example of his handling of the Bogo-Indian.

Game 11
Browne-Smyslov
Las Palmas (Interzonal) 1982

1	d4	♘f6
2	c4	e6
3	♘f3	♗b4+

4	♗d2	a5

Along with 4...c5, this is the most popular alternative to

4...♕e7. Apart from supporting the bishop, 4...a5 is a useful move in its own right: White will often wish to advance on the queenside with b2-b4, and ...a7-a5 acts as a useful pre-emptive move. It is bad for White to exchange on b4 since then Black has pressure down the half-open a-file with his rook; in addition, White has to be careful in playing a2-a3, since this leaves a hole on b3 which Black can play to exploit with ... a5-a4.

| 5 | g3 | d5 |

Attempting to take advantage of the fact that White has taken away the defence of c4 by fianchettoing his king's bishop. If White exchanges on d5, Black can recapture with his e-pawn and develop his queen's bishop easily.

6	♗g2	dxc4
7	♕c2	♘c6
8	♕xc4	♕d5

Black offers the exchange of queens. Again, if White exchanges on d5, Black can develop his queen's bishop; while if White does not exchange, the black queen can take up an active post on h5 or advance to e4 (see Chapter 6).

9	♕xd5	exd5
10	♘c3	♗e6
11	♖c1	a4

Black threatens to advance with ...a4-a3, forcing White to play b2-b3, after which White will have to be careful that Black cannot attack the pawn on a2. Browne elects to play a forcing line, but Smyslov has prepared a surprise.

12	♘b5	♗xd2+
13	♔xd2	♔d8
14	♘e5 *(D)*	

Now it would appear that Black is in some difficulties since 14...♘xe5 15 dxe5 ♘e8 16 f4 leaves White with the initiative, but Smyslov has something up his sleeve.

| 14 | ... | ♖a5 |

Now White can win material with 15 ♖xc6 ♖xb5 16 ♖xe6 fxe6 17 ♘f7+ ♔e7 18 ♘xh8 ♖xb2+

19 ♔d3 ♖xa2 20 ♖b1 b6 21 ♖c1 ♘e8, but then Black has very good compensation, since the white knight is trapped and Black already has two pawns for the piece. Browne is therefore forced to beat a hasty retreat.

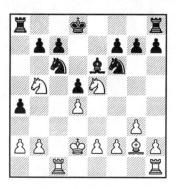

15	♘xc6+	bxc6
16	♘c3	♔e7

It is important to put the king here and not on d7: 16...♔d7 17 b3 axb3 18 axb3 ♖b8 19 ♘a4 and Black cannot capture on b3 because of 20 ♘c5+.

17	♘d1	♔d6
18	f3	c5
19	dxc5+	♖xc5
20	♖xc5	♔xc5
21	♘c3	♔b4

The black king protects the a-pawn and Black prepares to advance his d-pawn.

22	♖c1	c5
23	e3	d4
24	exd4	cxd4
25	a3+	♔b3
26	♘d1	♗c4

Preventing the white bishop from emerging via f1 and threatening ...♖e8.

27	♘f2	♘d5

27...♖e8 would be met by 28 ♗f1.

| 28 | ♘e4 | ♘e3 |

Now the black knight strangles White.

| 29 | ♘c5+ | ♔a2 |

White cannot take on a4 here since 30 ♘xa4 ♗b3 wins a piece. The black king is safe on a2 and White will eventually lose the b2 pawn.

30	♗h3	♗b3
31	♗d7	♘c4+
32	♔d3	0-1

White lost on time. After 32...♘e5+ 33 ♔xd4 ♘xd7 34 ♘xd7 ♖d8 35 ♖c7 ♗e6 wins a piece.

In the 1980s and early 1990s the major practitioners of the Bogo have been Korchnoi, Adams, Speelman, Seirawan, Christiansen, Andersson and Salov. To conclude this chapter we look at some examples from these contemporary players.

Game 12
Timman-Speelman
London 1982

1	d4	♘f6
2	c4	e6
3	♘f3	♗b4+
4	♗d2	♕e7
5	g3	♘c6
6	♕c2	

A slight divergence from the main line, but not one that should cause Black undue difficulties.

6	...	♗xd2+
7	♘bxd2	d6
8	♗g2	0-0
9	0-0	a5

As we have seen before, this is a useful prophylactic move, preventing White's expansion on the queenside with b2-b4.

10	e4	e5
11	d5	♘b8
12	♕c3	♘bd7
13	♘h4	

Although this a natural move, White could have tried instead to exchange off his bad bishop with 13 ♗h3, though even then Black has a satisfactory game after 13 ♗h3 ♘c5 14 ♗xc8 ♖hxc8 15 ♖fe1 c6.

13	...	♘c5
14	♖ae1	♗d7
15	b3	c6

The move ...c7-c6 is important for Black in this type of position. White does not normally exchange on c6, but retains the tension, but Black can then play ...cxd5 which can lead to pressure down the c-file or veiled threats along the e-file.

16	f4	♖fe8

Black is now threatening 17 ... exf4 18 gxf4 cxd5 when White cannot recapture with the e-pawn without losing two rooks for a queen. Since 19 cxd5 ♘xd5 wins a pawn for Black, Timman decides to relieve the tension, but this gives Black more freedom.

17	dxc6	bxc6
18	♔h1	exf4
19	♖xf4	

White is forced to play this re-capture, as 19 gxf4 ♘fxe4 20 ♘xe4 ♘xe4 21 ♖xe4 ♕xh4 wins a pawn. Black now has a good square for his pieces on e5.

19	...	♕e5
20	♕c2	♕d4

Black can play this move since 21 e5? loses to 21...♕d3. White should now continue with 21 ♗f1 with the probable continuation 21...♘g4 22 ♘hf3 ♘f2+ 23 ♔g1 ♘h3+ 24 ♔h1 ♘f2+ with a draw by perpetual check.

21	♘f1	a4
22	b4	

22 ♖d1 is better here; after 22...axb3 23 axb3 ♖a2 24 ♖xd4 ♖xc2 Black has a slight advantage Black because of White's disorganised pieces.

22	...	♕d3
23	♕c1	♘cxe4
24	♖e3	♕d4
25	a3	

After 25 ♗xe4 ♘xe4 26 ♘f3 Black escapes with 26...♕d1.

25	...	♖e7

The simple 25...d5 26 c5 ♕e5, with the idea of retreating the queen to c7, would have left Black a safe pawn up.

26	♘f3	

White could win the black queen for a rook and knight by 26 ♗xe4 ♖xe4 27 ♘f3 ♖xf4 28 ♘xd4 ♖xd4.

26	...	♕a7
27	♘g5	d5

28	♘xe4	dxe4

Now White cannot take the pawn on e4: 29 ♗xe4 ♖xe4 30 ♖fxe4 ♘xe4 31 ♖xe4 c5 and the long white diagonal is opened to effect.

29	♕c3	♘g4
30	♖e2	f5
31	♘d2	♕c7
32	♗h3	♘h6

32...h5 would have been better, keeping back the white army.

33	c5	♗e6
34	♘c4	♗xc4
35	♕xc4+	♔h8
36	♗xf5	♖f8

The critical position. Now White can play the extremely tactical 37 ♖exe4 with the brilliant point that after 37...♖xf5 38 ♖xf5 ♘xf5 he can reply 39 ♕f7 regaining the piece or 37...♘xf5 38 g4!. Timman missed this in time-trouble.

37	♖ef2	

Now Black really does win a piece.

37	...	g5
38	♖xe4	♖xf5

39	♕d4+	♔g8
40	♕c4+	♖ff7
41	♖fe2	♖xe4
42	♖xe4	♕d7
43	♖d4	♕e7
44	♖e4	♕f6
45	g4	♕f3+
46	♔g1	♕f2+
47	♔h1	♔f8
48	♕d3	♖d7
49	♕e2	♕xe2

50	♖xe2	♘g8
51	♖e5	♘e7
52	♔g2	♖d3
	0-1	

In the 1980s Korchnoi and Salov developed a new system based on 4... c5 in the 4 ♗d2 variation, and this soon became established as a dynamic alternative to the old 4...♕e7.

Game 13
Kasparov-Korchnoi
Brussels (OHRA) 1986

1	d4	♘f6
2	c4	e6
3	♘f3	♗b4+
4	♗d2	c5
5	g3	

Probably not the best response; White does better to exchange on b4 (see the next game).

5	...	♕b6
6	♗g2	♘c6

White now chooses to sacrifice a pawn for speedy development.

7	d5	exd5
8	cxd5	♘xd5
9	0-0	♘de7
10	e4	d6
11	♗e3	♕c7
12	a3	♗a5
13	♗f4	

Here 13 ♘bd2 gives White more chances (see Chapter 7).

| 13 | ... | ♘e5 |

Black has been able to defend his backward d-pawn, but typically Kasparov conjures up another pawn sacrifice before his opponent can consolidate .

14	b4	cxb4
15	axb4	♗xb4
16	♕a4+	♘7c6
17	♘d4	a5

Black defends his bishop against the threat of ♗xe5. However, it was more accurate to play 17...♗c5, not allowing the white knight to remain on d4.

18   ♘c3   ♗d7

After 18...♗xc3 19 ♘b5 ♕d8 20 ♘xc3 0-0 21 ♖fd1 White has some compensation for the material deficit.

19	♘d5	♕d8
20	♘f5	0-0
21	♕d1	♗c5
22	♖c1	a4
23	g4	a3
24	g5	a2
25	♕h5	♗xf5

Black could have sacrificed his queen by 25...♘d3 26 ♘f6+ gxf6 27 ♕h6 ♗xf5 28 gxf6 ♕xf6 29 ♕xf6 ♘xc1 30 ♖xc1 ♗g6 31 ♗h6 ♗d4 when he has a winning advantage, but this was very hard to see. The rest of the game was played in severe time-trouble for both sides.

26	exf5	♗d4
27	♗xe5	♘xe5
28	♗e4	♖e8
29	♖c7	a1(♕)
30	♖xa1	♖xa1+
31	♔g2	♖a2

If 31...♘g6 32 fxg6 fxg6 33 ♗xg6 hxg6 34 ♕xg6 White has

the threat of ♕f7+ with a draw by perpetual check.

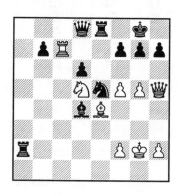

32   ♖e7

If 32 f6 ♘g6 33 ♗xg6 hxg6 34 ♘e7+ ♕xe7 35 ♖xe7 gxh5 36 ♖xe8+ ♔h7 wins for Black.

32	...	♖xf2+
33	♔g3	♖xe7
34	f6	♘g6?

34...h6 35 ♘xe7+ ♔f8 should win for Black.

35	♘xe7+	♔f8
36	♕xh7	♗xf6

Another chance goes begging: 36...gxf6! 37 ♗xg6 fxg6 38 ♘xg6+ ♔e8 wins.

37	♘xg6+	fxg6
38	♔xf2?	

White misses a chance to force a draw with 38 ♗d5! ♗e5+ 39 ♔xf2 ♕xg5 40 ♕g8+ ♔e7 41 ♕f7+ ♔d8.

38	...	♕b6+?

Black could still a big advantage with 38...♗d4+ 39 ♔e2 ♕xg5.

39	♔g2	♕b2+
40	♔h3	♗xg5?

Better was 40...♗e5 and if 41

♕xg6 ♕xh2+ 42 ♔g4 ♕g3+ 43 ♔f5 ♕h3 mate.

41   ♕xg6   ♕f6

41...♗f6 42 ♗d5 ♕c3+ would still leave Black some winning chances.

½-½

The next game shows White exchanging on b4 immediately, which is now established as the main line of the 4...c5 variation.

Game 14
Adorjan-Salov
Szirak (Interzonal) 1987

1	d4	♘f6
2	♘f3	e6
3	c4	♗b4+
4	♗d2	c5
5	♗xb4	cxb4
6	g3	b6
7	♗g2	♗b7
8	0-0	0-0
9	♘bd2	

White is forced by the pawn on b4 to develop the knight on this rather passive square. The other course of action would be to play an early a2-a3 to exchange the annoying pawn on b4 (see Chapter 7).

9	...	a5
10	♖e1	d6
11	e4 *(D)*	

White has an impressive pawn centre, but Black can establish a strongpoint on e5, which in turn may allow him to reposition his king's knight on c5 at a later stage of the game.

11	...	♘fd7
12	♕c2	e5
13	♖ad1	♘c6
14	♘f1	♕c7
15	♘e3	♘e7

16	dxe5	dxe5
17	♘d5	♘xd5
18	exd5	♖ae8
19	♘g5	g6
20	b3	♘c5
21	h4	♕d6
22	♖d2	♗c8
23	♕d1	♔g7
24	♕a1	♗f5
25	f4	f6
26	fxe5	♖xe5
27	♖xe5	♕xe5
28	♕xe5	fxe5

The black knight remains on its fine outpost on c5 from which it can support the advance of the black passed e-pawn, while restraining the passed white d-pawn.

29	♔h2	h6
30	♘h3	e4
31	d6	♖d8
32	♘f4	g5
33	♘e2	♗g4
34	♘c1	e3
35	♖d5	e2
36	♖e5	♔f6
37	♖e3	♖xd6
38	♘xe2	♖d2

39	♘c1	♖d1
40	♘e2	♖d2
41	♘c1	♔g6
	0-1	

White is in zugzwang: he cannot move a piece without losing.

The 4 ♗d2 a5 has also seen some fresh ideas in recent years; Black has developed more ambitious systems, allowing him to make a real fight for the initiative, as we see in the next game.

Game 15
Adianto-Christiansen
San Francisco 1991

1	d4	♘f6
2	♘f3	e6
3	c4	♗b4+
4	♗d2	a5
5	g3	d6
6	♗g2	♘bd7
7	0-0	e5
8	e3	♗xd2

The ever-enterprising Christiansen also examined sacrificing his bishop on b4 with 8...♕e7!? 9 ♗c1 e4 10 ♘g5 h6 11 ♘h3 (11 ♘xe4 ♘xe4 12 a3 ♗c5 13 dxc5 ♘dxc5 with good play for Black due to his active knights) 11...d5 12 c5 g5!?.

9	♕xd2	0-0
10	♘c3	♕e7
11	♖fd1	♖e8
12	♘b5?!	

This knight thrust allows Black to gain control of the central light squares. 12 ♖ac1 or 12 e4 would have been more appropriate.

12   ...   ♘f8

Not 12...♘b6?! 13 c5 dxc5 14 dxe5 ♘g4 15 ♕c3 when White has a good game because of Black's weak queenside pawns.

13   c5

13   ...   e4
14   cxd6   cxd6
15   ♘e1   ♗g4

This drives the rook where it wants to go; 15...♗f5 with the idea of ...♘e6 was a better alternative.

16   ♖dc1   ♘e6
17   ♖c2

After 17 h3? ♗f5 leaves White with a weakness on h3 which Black can exploit with ...♕d7, and ...h7-h5.   17 b4!?, intending to generate counterplay on the queenside, was worth consideration.

17   ...   ♕d7
18   a4   ♘g5!?

Black bravely goes full ahead for the kingside attack. The safe alternative was 18...♗f5! with the

idea of ...♘d5 stopping any invasions on the queenside. White could reply 19 b4 axb4 20 ♕xb4 ♖a6 when the chances are balanced.

19   ♘c7

White takes up the challenge and wins the exchange but he had little choice: 19 ♖c7 ♕e6 20 ♖xb7 ♗f3! 21 ♘c7 ♘h3+ 22 ♔h1 ♕f5 23 ♘xe8 ♖xe8 leaves White defenceless against the threat of ...♘g4 and ...♘gxf2+.

19   ...   ♗f3
20   ♘xf3

This allows Black to win two pieces for a rook. The critical alternative   was 20 ♘xe8 to which   Black   should   reply 20...♖xe8 21 ♕xa5 ♕g4, when Christiansen looks at two possibilities:

a) 22 h4 ♘h3+ 23 ♔h2 ♗xg2 24 ♘xg2 g5 25 ♕b5 (25 hxg5 ♘xg5 26 ♘f4 ♘h5 wins) 25...h5 26 ♕e2 ♕f5 27 hxg5 ♘xg5 28 ♘f4 ♘d5! 29 ♕b5 ♖e5!! 30 dxe5 ♘xf4 when White is unable to stop ...♕h3+ and ...♘f3 mate;

b) 22 ♘xf3 exf3 23 ♗f1 h5 24 h4 ♘h3+ 25 ♔h2 ♘xf2 26 ♖xf2 ♘e4 27 ♖xf3 ♕xf3 28 ♕e1 ♘f2! and Black has a raging attack.

20   ...   exf3
21   ♘xe8

After 21 ♗h1 ♕h3 22 ♕d1 ♘g4 23 ♗xf3 ♕xh2+ 24 ♔f1 ♖xe3! (24...♘xf3 25 ♕xf3 ♘xe3 also wins) 25 ♘xa8 g6 26 ♗g2 ♘h3! 27 fxe3 ♕g1+ 28 ♔e2 ♕xe3+ 29 ♔f1 ♘h2 White is checkmated (Christiansen).

Instead 21 &f1 &h3+ 22 &h1 &e4 23 ♕e1 &exf2 leads to a more prosaic win for Black.

21	...	&h3+
22	&h1	fxg2+
23	&xg2	♖xe8
24	♕xa5	d5

The situation has crystallised: Black has two pieces for a rook and two pawns, but more important is his strong attack against the white king.

25	♖ac1	h5
26	♕b5	♕f5
27	♕e2	&g5
28	f3	

28	...	h4
29	gxh4	

If White tries to avoid the break up of his kingside then Black can win by sacrificing his knight 29 g4 &xg4! 30 fxg4 ♕e4+ 31 &f2 &h3+ 32 &e1 &f4! 33 exf4 ♕h1+ 34 &d2 ♖xe2+ 35 &xe2 ♕xh2+ with a winning endgame for Black (Christiansen).

29	...	♕h3+
30	&h1	&xf3
31	♕g2	♕xg2+
32	&xg2	♖xe3
33	♖c3	&xh4+
34	&f1	♖e4
35	♖b3	♖f4+!
36	&g1	

After 36 &e2 &e4 37 ♖c8+ (not 37 ♖xb7 ♖f2+ 38 &d3 ♖d2+ 39 &e3 &g2+ 40 &f3 ♖f2+ 41 &g4 f5+ 42 &h5 &f4+ 43 &h4 g5 mate) 37...&h7 38 ♖xb7 &d6 wins material (Christiansen).

36	...	&e4
37	♖xb7	♖f2
38	♖b3	♖g2+
	0-1	

A brilliant win by Christiansen.

The following gem also illustrates how Black can spring into action if White plays too passively.

Game 16
Lputian-Petursson
Lucerne (World Team Championship) 1993

1	d4	&f6
2	c4	e6
3	&f3	&b4+
4	&bd2	b6

5	e3	&b7
6	&d3	0-0
7	0-0	d5
8	a3	&xd2

Petursson's new move, and one that seems to promise excellent chances of equality. After the old 8...♗d6 or 8...♗e7 White can play 9 b4!, discouraging the freeing ...c7-c5.

9	♗xd2	dxc4
10	♗xc4	♘bd7
11	♕e2	c5

A typical position from the 4 ♘bd2 line. White has the two bishops and long-term prospects if he can use the bishop pair in the endgame, but Black has active play for his minor pieces.

12	♖fd1	♕e7
13	dxc5	♘xc5

Black has a grip on the e4 square, which makes it difficult for White to break out.

14	♘d4	♘fe4
15	f3	♘xd2
16	♖xd2	a6
17	b4	♘d7
18	♕f2	♘e5
19	♗f1	♖ac8
20	e4	♖c3!

Petursson increases his control on the game, preparing to double

rooks on the c-file and eyeing the a3 pawn. White is tempted to drive away the rook but runs into some tactical fireworks; he had to try 21 ♖c2.

21	♘e2?

21	...	♖xf3!
22	♕xb6	

After 22 gxf3 ♕g5+ 23 ♘g3 ♕xd2 24 ♕xd2 ♘xf3+ 25 ♔f2 ♘xd2 Black is two pawns up.

22	...	♕g5
23	♕xb7	♖h3!!

A brilliant move, putting the rook on another attacked square.

24	♕a7

If White plays 24 ♖ad1, Black forces checkmate as follows 24...♕e3+ 25 ♔h1 ♖xh2+ 26 ♔xh2 ♘g4+ 27 ♔h1 ♕h6+ 28 ♔g1 ♕h2 mate, whilst 24 ♔h1 is met by 24...♖xh2+ 25 ♔xh2 ♕h4+ 26 ♔g1 ♘g4 27 ♕c7 e5 and 24 ♔f2 by 24...♕h4+ 25 g3 ♕f6+ 26 ♔g2 ♘g4! 27 ♔xh3 ♘e3 (Petursson).

24	...	♘f3+
25	♔f2	♘xd2
	0-1	

Since 26 gxh3 ♕f6 is curtains.

This concludes our historical survey of the Bogo-Indian. In the next chapter we shall examine some of the positional themes that are critical to understanding this opening.

Positional Themes

The previous chapter introduced some of the characteristics of the Bogo-Indian from a historical perspective. Before moving on to a specific analysis of the individual variations, it is worthwhile discussing some of the positional features of the opening as you will find that certain themes recur in different lines.

White has the two bishops
The Bogo-Indian is similar to the Nimzo-Indian Defence, in that Black is often obliged to surrender his king's bishop for a knight:

After **1 d4 ♘f6 2 c4 e6 3 ♘f3 ♗b4+ 4 ♘bd2**

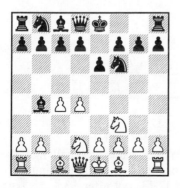

We can see why Black often must surrender his king's bishop for the white knight on d2. White may play a2-a3 when Black must exchange or retreat his king's bishop; but even if White does not play a2-a3, choosing to develop and castle kingside then the black king's bishop is not usefully placed on b4.

At first sight it seems that after 4 ♘bd2 White has the advantage, because Black will have to exchange off the king's bishop or retreat. In fact, the retreat is often playable, since the white knight is not aggressively placed and Black is not under great pressure in the centre; and if Black does exchange then he can use the time gained by his speedy development to stake a claim in the centre. The first three moves of the Bogo-Indian 1... ♘f6, 2...e6, 3...♗b4+ enable Black to castle immediately, and he is well placed to counterattack in the centre with ...d7-d5 and/or ...c7-c5.

Black may also be forced to give up the two bishops after the following sequence:

1	d4	♘f6
2	c4	e6

3   ♘f3   ♗b4+
4   ♗d2   ♕e7
5   ♘c3

Here Black has no retreat of the king's bishop and has to exchange on c3 in some positions. We shall commence our examination of the two bishops theme from this position.

Game 17
Vidmar-Nimzowitsch
New York 1927

(1 d4 ♘f6 2 c4 e6 3 ♘f3 ♗b4+ 4 ♗d2 ♕e7 5 ♘c3)

5   ...   0-0
6   e3   d6

Black has two ways of playing this position: he can either fianchetto his queen's bishop by ...b7-b6 and ...♗b7 and aim to create an outpost on e4 for his knight; or play for ...e7-e5.

7   ♗e2

After 7 ♗d3 e5 is good, since White must lose time attending to the threat of 8...♗xc3 followed by 9...e4 winning a piece.

7   ...   b6

Now Black will establish good control of the light squares in the centre, particularly e4.

8   0-0   ♗b7
9   ♕c2   ♘bd7
10   ♖ad1   ♗xc3
11   ♗xc3   ♘e4

Black's strategy gradually reveals itself; he is going to build up a kingside attack using his outpost on e4.

12   ♗e1   f5
13   ♕b3

White wants to challenge the black steed on e4 by playing ♘d2 and f2-f3, but after 13 ♘d2 ♕g5 14 f3 is not possible due to ...

♕xe3+, so White prepares this by protecting his e-pawn.

13 ... c5

This is very useful later on as White otherwise might be able to play c4-c5 with effect.

14	♘d2	♘xd2
15	♖xd2	e5
16	dxe5	dxe5
17	f3	g5

Black starts his attack and would like to open up the long diagonal to White's king by ... g5-g4. Meanwhile, White can try to create counterplay down the d-file.

18	♗f2	♘f6
19	♖fd1	♖ae8
20	♕a4	♗a8
21	♖d6	

21 ♖d7 ♘xd7 22 ♖xd7 ♕f6 23 ♕xa7 ♖f7 is insufficient for White.

| 21 | ... | ♕g7 |
| 22 | ♗f1 | |

Too meek; 22 ♗e1 is much better after 22...g4 23 fxg4 ♘xg4 24 ♖d7 ♕g5 25 ♗xg4 ♕xg4 26 ♕c2 ♗e4 with a slight advantage for Black.

| 22 | ... | e4 |
| 23 | ♗e1 | |

Or 23 f4 gxf4 24 exf4 e3.

23	...	exf3
24	♗c3	♕e7
25	♖6d3	

White's intended 25 ♗xf6 loses to 25...♕xe3+ 26 ♔h1 fxg2+ 27 ♗xg2 ♕e1+ 28 ♖xe1 ♖xe1 mate.

25	...	fxg2
26	♗xg2	♗xg2
27	♗xf6	♕e4
28	♖1d2	♗h3
29	♗c3	♕g4+
	0-1	

Black mates in two.

This is a model game to study, but White's play was insipid and Vidmar allowed Black too much of a free hand on the kingside. White should fight for control of the central light squares, as shown in this brilliant demonstration by Portisch.

Game 18
Portisch-Andersson
London 1982

| 1 | d4 | ♘f6 | | 2 | c4 | e6 |

3	♘f3	♗b4+
4	♘bd2	b6
5	e3	c5
6	a3	♗xd2+
7	♕xd2	

White takes with the queen in order to fianchetto his queen's bishop.

| 7 | ... | 0-0 |
| 8 | ♗e2 | a5 |

Andersson was probably afraid of White expanding on the queenside with b2-b4, but this move may be weakening in the long term. Black could consider 8...♗a6 with the idea of playing ...d7-d5 and exchanging the light-squared bishops. White could try to prevent this by 9 b4 d5 10 b5 ♗b7, but Black then has a satisfactory game because of his control of e4.

| 9 | b3 | ♗b7 |
| 10 | 0-0 | d6 |

This allows Portisch to carry out a neat manoeuvre to gain control of the central light squares, which could have been prevented by 10...♘e4.

| 11 | ♖d1 | |

Portisch plans to retreat his queen to e1 if the black knight leaps to e4, and then evict the knight with ♘d2.

11	...	♘bd7
12	♗b2	♘e4
13	♕e1	♕e7
14	♘d2	♘xd2
15	♕xd2	

White has neutralized Black's attacking chances on the kingside while retaining the bishop pair, and will eventually open up the game for his two bishops.

| 15 | ... | ♖fd8 |
| 16 | ♕c3 | ♘f6 |

The wrong plan. Black should attempt to block the diagonal of the white queen's bishop by 16...e5, possibly with a later ...f7-f6.

| 17 | f3 | |

The key move; White controls e4 and d5 with pawns and the black minor pieces are restricted.

17	...	d5
18	dxc5	bxc5
19	♖ac1	♖dc8

20	♕e5	♕c7

A better chance was 20...♕f8, though White still has a big advantage. Now White has a terrific bind in the ending.

21	♕xc7	♖xc7
22	♗e5	♖cc8
23	cxd5	♗xd5
24	♖c3	

Already Black is having trouble defending the weak pawns and squares in his position.

24	...	♘d7
25	♗g3	a4
26	e4	

Not 26 bxa4 ♘b6 when Black is well placed.

24	...	♗c6
27	b4	cxb4
28	axb4	

The black minor pieces are skating on thin ice: the bishop is exposed and the knight is wandering around looking for a safe post.

28	...	♘f6
29	b5	♗b7
30	♖a3	♘h5
31	♗f2	♘f4
32	♗f1	g5
33	g3	♘g6
34	♖d7	♖cb8
35	♗d4	g4
36	♗a1	h5
37	♗e2	♖a5
38	♔f2	♖aa8
39	♔e3	gxf3
40	♗xf3	♘f8
41	♖c7	♗c8
42	e5	♖a5
43	♗c6	1-0

Black cannot move a piece and is helpless against the threat of 44 ♗c3.

Portisch's handling of the white side was superb; he exchanged off Black's aggressive knight on e4 and then took control of e4 by f2-f3. Black must play actively in this line and try to create attacking chances on the kingside. The following game is a good illustration of Black's strategy in these positions.

Game 19
Dahlberg-Korchnoi
Lone Pine 1981

1	d4	♘f6		3	♘f3	♗b4+
2	c4	e6		4	♘bd2	c5

This move commits Black to an exchange of his king's bishop for White's queen knight.

5	a3	♗xd2+
6	♕xd2	b6
7	e3	♗b7
8	♗e2	♘c6

Why does Korchnoi develop his knight on c6 blocking the diagonal of his queen's bishop, when he could have developed the knight on d7 by playing ...d7-d6? Because the queen's knight would have been passively placed on d7, whereas on c6 it has a future via e7 and g6.

9	0-0	0-0
10	b3	♘e4
11	♕c2	f5

Black stakes his claim on the e4 square, ...f7-f5 is also a useful move since Black can later manoeuvre his rook into the attack via f6.

12	♖d1	♘e7
13	dxc5	bxc5
14	♗b2	

Again control of e4 is of paramount importance. White should continue with 15 ♘e5 or 14 ♘d2 with the idea of driving the Black steed away with f2-f3.

14	...	d6
15	♘d2	♘g6
16	♗f3	

This exposes White to a lethal attack down the long diagonal. On 16 f3 ♕g5 17 ♘f1 ♘h4 18 g3 ♘f6 White has considerable weaknesses on the kingside but 16 ♘f1 would have been much better.

| 16 | ... | ♘h4 |
| 17 | ♗xe4 | |

17 ♘xe4 ♘xf3+ 18 gxf3 fxe4 19 f4 ♕e7 leaves Black with a clear advantage, but it is White's best choice.

| 17 | ... | fxe4 |
| 18 | ♘xe4 (D) | |

White exposes himself to a devastating blow; 18 ♘f1 is not without hope.

| 18 | ... | ♘xg2 |
| 19 | ♕c3 | |

Here 19 ♔xg2 ♕h4 20 f3 ♖xf3 21 ♔xf3 ♖f8+ 22 ♔e2 ♗xe4 is decisive.

19   ...   ♕e7

20	♘xd6	♗f3
21	♖d2	♘h4
22	♕e5	♗e2
	0-1	

23...♘f3 is terminal.

Black can also attempt a different strategy against 4 ♘bd2: first exchange on d2 and then play for ...e6-e5 with ...d7-d6 and ...♕e7. While this approach should be sufficient to equalize, it does open the position in favour of White's bishops.

Game 20
P. Littlewood-Short
Hastings 1981

1	d4	♘f6
2	c4	e6
3	♘f3	♗b4+
4	♘bd2	0-0
5	e3	d6

Black commits himself to exchanging his king's bishop.

| 6 | a3 | ♗xd2+ |
| 7 | ♗xd2 | ♕e7 |

Black prepares to play ...e6-e5 opening up the c8-h3 diagonal for his bishop.

8	♕c2	e5
9	dxe5	dxe5
10	♗c3	

White puts more pressure on the exposed black e-pawn. It is bad for Black to advance with 10

...e4 since after 11 ②d2 his pawn is even more vulnerable and White's dark-squared bishop dominates the whole board.

10   ...   ②bd7

Simic recommends 10...②c6 11 b4 ♗g4 12 b5 ♗xf3 13 gxf3 ②d4 with equality, but White can play more slowly with 11 h3, followed by ♗e2, with good prospects because of the bishop pair.

11   g4

A very aggressive move; White could have retained a slight advantage with 11 ♗e2, but instead tries for a direct attack.

11   ...   b6

Capturing the g-pawn is very dangerous: after 11...②xg4 12 ♖g1 White has a ready-made attack down the g-file.

12   ♖g1   ♗b7
13   ②d2   ②c5
14   b4   ②e6

Black offers White a pawn, but if White takes on e5 then Black can seize the initiative by 15 ♗xe5 a5 16 b5 ②d7 17 ♗c3

②dc5 when Black has positional compensation for the pawn.

15   g5   ②d7
16   ♗d3   g6

Not 16...②xg5 17 h4, followed by 18 ♗xh7+ opening up the black king.

17   ♗e4

A fine move. White offers the exchange of light-squared bishops in order to exchange the e4 square for the knight. If Black declines by 17...c6 then White can continue in aggressive vein with 18 h4.

17   ...   ♗xe4
18   ②xe4   a5
19   ♖d1

White threatens to win immediately with 20 ♖xd7 and 21 ②f6+.

19   ...   ♖fd8
20   ♖xd7   ♖xd7
21   ②f6+   ♔f8
22   ♕e4   ♖ad8

The best defence; 22...♖dd8 23 ②xh7+ ♔e8 24 ♕c6+ wins for White.

23   ②xh7+   ♔g8

24	♘f6+	♕xf6
25	gxf6	♖d1+
26	♔e2	♖xg1
27	bxa5	bxa5
28	h4	

An important move, taking away the g5 square from the black rook.

28	...	a4
29	♕xe5	♖g4
30	♕b5	♖xh4

Although White obtains a passed a-pawn, Black can conjure enough counterplay by attacking the white king.

31	♕xa4	♖h1
32	♕c2	♘g5
33	a4	♘h3

The knight is surprisingly mobile here.

| 34 | ♕e4 | ♖c1 |

Black threatens 35...♘g1 mate, which forces White to retreat his bishop to a passive position.

35	♗e1	♘g5
36	♕e7	♖c2+
37	♔f1	♘e6
38	♔g2	♖xc4
39	a5	♖c1
40	♗b4	c5
41	♗a3	♖a1
	½-½	

The queenside pawns are liquidated after 42 ♗xc5 ♖xa5 43 ♗b6 ♖g5+ 44 ♔f3 ♖b8 when the chances are evenly balanced.

A good fighting game, but one that illustrates the dangers for Black, who should always try to limit the scope of White's two bishops.

Static pawn chains

In the line 1 d4 ♘f6 2 c4 e6 3 ♘f3 ♗b4+ 4 ♗d2 ♕e7 the central position can often become blocked after the exchange of dark-squared bishops, with a pawn structure like this.

It is worthwhile examining this position, which we have already seen in the Timman-Speelman game in the previous chapter, since it is very typical. White has a choice of pawn breaks: he can either go for a queenside push with b2-b4 and c4-c5 or a kingside thrust with f2-f4. Black can similarly attack the head of White's pawn chain with ...c7-c6 or the base with ...f7-f5. In practice Black normally has difficulty in engineering ...f7-f5 without a great deal of regrouping, but the break ...c7-c6 is often very useful for Black. If White exchanges on c6 then Black's central control is increased after ...bxc6. If White keeps the tension, Black often opens the position advantageously with ...cxd5.

Game 21
Martin-Taulbut
London 1980

1	d4	♘f6
2	c4	e6
3	♘f3	♗b4+
4	♗d2	♕e7
5	g3	♘c6
6	♗g2	♗xd2+
7	♘bxd2	0-0
8	0-0	d6
9	e4	a5

This move allows White to advance with 10 e5, but Black has a satisfactory position after that as we shall see in Chapter 9.

10	♕e2	e5
11	d5	♘b8

Here we have a very similar pawn chain to that discussed above. White now prepares f2-f4.

12	♘h4	c6

Why is this such an important move? The effect is seen after 13 f4 exf4 14 ♖xf4 cxd5 when White loses a pawn after 15 cxd5 ♘xd5 due to the pin on the e-file.

White could protect his queen by ♖ae1, but then Black could renew this theme with ...♖e8.

13	♖ac1	♘a6

Black develops smoothly; the knight will come to c5 and the bishop to d7.

14	h3	♗d7

White is now hard-pushed to find a constructive plan, since Black has prevented f2-f4 and it will take White a long time to prepare b2-b4 and c4-c5.

15	dxc6	bxc6
16	♘f5	♗xf5
17	exf5	

White is hoping to build up an attack on the kingside and along the e-file, but Black has a sound position.

17	...	♖ac8
18	♘b3	

White tries to deflect Black by attacking the black queenside pawns, but this should not trouble Black.

18	...	a4
19	♘a5	e4
20	♕c2	♕c7

20...♘c5 21 b4 axb3 22 axb3 ♘d3 23 ♖cd1 d5 leaves White with problems.

21	♕xa4	♘c5
22	♕a3	♖a8
23	b4	♘d3
24	♖cd1	c5

The rook manoeuvre 24...♖fb8 comes seriously into consideration.

25	♖xd3	exd3
26	♗xa8	♖xa8
27	♕xd3	cxb4
28	♘b3	♖xa2
29	♖d1	h5

White should now play 30 ♕xd6 as 30...♕xc4 loses to 31 ♕b8+ ♔h7 32 ♖d8, so Black would have to continue with 30...♕xd6 31 ♖xd6 with an equal ending.

30	♖b1	♘d7
31	♕d5	♕b6
32	c5	♘xc5
33	♘xc5	♖a5
34	♘d7	♕c7
35	♘f6+	gxf6
36	♕f3	♕c3
37	♕b7	♖a1
38	♖xa1	♕xa1+
39	♔g2	♕d4
	0-1	

Here is another typical example of this line.

Game 22
P. Littlewood-Taulbut
Charlton 1983

1	d4	♘f6
2	c4	e6
3	♘f3	♗b4+
4	♗d2	♕e7
5	♕c2	

The usual move is 5 g3; but White chooses to prepare e2-e4.

5	...	♗xd2+
6	♘bxd2	d6
7	g3	e5

8	♗g2

An interesting position. White is inviting Black to press on with ...e5-e4 followed by ...e4-e3, but White is better developed and this opening of the position is advantageous for him: 8...e4 9 ♘g5 e3 10 ♘de4 ♘xe4 11 ♘xe4 exf2+ 12 ♘xf2 ♕e3 13 ♕d2 and White's powerful bishop gives him the edge.

| 8 | ... | 0-0 |
| 9 | 0-0 | a5 |

Again 9...e4 10 ♘g5 e3 11 ♘de4 opens the position for White's pieces. The text is a useful waiting move, because if the centre becomes blocked with White playing d4-d5 Black will be able to restrain his opponent's queenside pawn advance.

10	♕c3	♖e8
11	d5	♘bd7
12	e4	♘c5
13	♖ae1	

A typical position from this line of the Bogo-Indian; White is planning a kingside push with f4 and Black a ...c7-c6 break.

| 13 | ... | c6 |

A very useful move, giving Black the option of opening up the c-file with ...cxd5.

| 14 | ♘h4 | ♗d7 |

Now Black has possibilities of ...b7-b5 and exchanging on d5, so White releases the tension by exchanging on c6. However, this merely increases

Black's central control.

| 15 | dxc6 | bxc6 |
| 16 | h3? | |

The best plan was 16 b3, with the idea of driving the black knight away with a2-a3 and b2-b4.

| 16 | ... | h6?! |

Black should have played 16...a4, which would have prevented the plan of a2-a3 and b2-b4; 17 b4 axb3 18 axb3 ♖a3 would then leave Black with good play.

| 17 | b3 | ♘h5 |

It is difficult for Black to undertake a positive plan, but this move allows White to play his knight to f5.

| 18 | ♘f5 | ♕f8 |

18...♗xf5 19 exf5 ♖ec8 20 f4 is good for White, so Black has to retreat.

| 19 | ♘b1 | |

White prepares to put pressure against the black d-pawn.

| 19 | ... | ♘f6 |

Black realizes his mistake and repositions his knight on the good square f6, preventing a double attack on the d-pawn as 20 ♖d1 and 20 ♕d2 are bad because of 20...♘xe4.

| 20 | g4 | |

A dubious move which weakens the f4 square.

20	...	g6
21	♘g3	♘e6
22	♘e2	g5
23	♕d2	c5

The central position has become clarified. Black has the

better prospects because his bishop has more scope than White's and the weak d6 pawn can be shielded by planting a knight on d4.

24 ②bc3 h5!?
This double-edged move sparks off some interesting complications. Safe and good was the positional 24...②d4.
25 h4!

This is White's best try. The passive 25 f3 leaves the bishop without much hope of escape and 25 gxh5 ②xh5 is also bad since Black will establish a powerful

knight on f4.
5 ... hxg4
26 hxg5 ②h5
Sounder was 26...②h7 27 ②d5 ♕g7 with advantage to Black as the g-pawn will fall.
27 ②d5 ♕g7
As planned, but now Black gets a shock.
28 ②g3
Trouble looms for Black, since he cannot exchange knights without the f6 square becoming drastically weak. Black is now forced to enter tactical complications in which he may have to sacrifice the exchange.
28 ... ②ef4
29 ②xh5 ②xh5
Now White can take the exchange, but this leads to Black obtaining a very strong kingside attack, e.g. 30 ②c7 ②f4 31 ②xa8 ♕xg5 32 ♕xd6 ②h3+ 33 ♔h1 ♖e6 34 ♕xd7 ♖h6 35 ♗xh3 ♖xh3+ 36 ♔g2 ♕f4 37 ♖g1 ♖h2+ 38 ♔f1 ♕xf2 mate. So White spurns the offered material in favour of active play.
30 f4 ♗e6
The best choice for Black here; 30...exf4 31 ②f6+ ②xf6 32 gxf6 ♕xf6 33 e5 wins for White.
31 fxe5
Taking the exchange is bad: 31 ②c7 ②xf4 32 ②xa8 ♖xa8 33 ♕xd6 ♕xg5 and Black has a superb position because of his massive knight on f4 and possibilities of a kingside attack.
31 ... ♗xd5
32 exd5 ♖xe5

33	♖xe5	♛xe5
34	♖e1	

Black has weathered the storm and has a slight initiative, because White's bishop on g2 has hardly any scope. White has one major piece extra in play, but Black can seize the initiative with 34...♛g3!. Instead he plays a safe move that allows White good drawing chances.

34	...	♛f4?
35	♛xf4	♘xf4
36	♖e4	♘d3
37	♖xg4	♘c1
38	♖e4	♘xa2
39	♖e7	♘c1
40	♖b7	♘e2+
41	♔f2	♘d4

Black still has some winning chances if he can activate his king, but White's next move prevents this.

42	♗e4	♖e8
43	♗d3	♔f8
44	♖b6	♖d8
45	♖b7	♖e8
46	♖b6	♖d8
47	♖b7	½-½

Now it is too risky for either side to try and win.

A good game with many interesting points. Further examples with this formation can be found in Chapter 9.

Black's queenside fianchetto

We have already seen some important examples of the queenside fianchetto in this chapter. In Vidmar-Nimzowitsch Black's fianchetto bishop controlled the light squares in the centre, but in Portisch-Andersson White took over these squares and denied Black the use of the e4 square by playing f3, which proved to be the decisive factor. Here we see a situation in which Black can play his queen's bishop to a6 instead.

Game 23
Pritchett-Taulbut
London 1981

1	d4	♘f6	5	a3	♗xd2+
2	c4	e6	6	♛xd2 (D)	
3	♘f3	♗b4+	6	...	b6
4	♘bd2	0-0	7	g3	c5

Black must play aggressively in this position, since otherwise he will have no compensation for White's two bishops; this pawn thrust is better than 7...d5 8 ♘e5 followed by 9 ♗g2. White cannot now advance in the centre with 8 d5 exd5 9 cxd5 because 9...♗b7 is very strong.

8 ♗g2 ♘c6

Black does not yet develop his queen's bishop in order to retain the option of placing it on a6.

9 0-0

Instead 9 ♘e5 cxd4 10 ♗xc6 dxc6 11 ♘xc6 ♕c7 12 ♘xd4 ♕xc4 is fine for Black.

9 ... ♗a6

The key to Black's play is pressure on the a6-f1 diagonal; 9...♗b7 10 dxc5 bxc5 11 b4 would be pleasant for White.

10 b3 d5

Black gives himself hanging pawns, but has good piece play in return; so a dynamic equilibrium is reached.

11	cxd5	exd5
12	dxc5	bxc5

Now the battle begins. White hopes to weaken and pick off the hanging pawns, and Black aims to press down the b- and e-files.

13	♗b2	♘e4
14	♕c2	♕b6
15	♖ad1	♖ad8
16	♘e5	♘xe5
17	♗xe5	♕g6

Black now has the tactical threat of 18...♘xg3 and 18 ♖fe1 ♕f5 does not help matters.

18	♖xd5	♘xg3
19	♕xg6	♘xe2+
20	♔h1	hxg6
21	♖xc5	♖fe8

White still has the two bishops and a queenside majority, but his kingside is wrecked.

22	♖a5	♖e6
23	♖e1	♘f4
24	♖xa6	♖xe5

Unfortunately for White he cannot take the rook because of mate.

| 25 | ♖f1 | ♖d3 |
| 26 | ♖xa7 | ♖g5? |

A mistake; better was the simple 26...♖xb3 with very good chances. White's a-pawn is not as dangerous as Black's kingside play.

| 27 | ♗e4 | ♖d4 |
| 28 | ♖e1?? | |

White has a difficult task, but 28 ♗f3 is much better.

28	...	♖e5
29	♖a4	♖exe4
	0-1	

Whichever rook is taken, it is mate next move. An interesting game showing the vitality of Black's position in this line.

The idea of playing the bishop to a6 instead of b7 can also be played in other lines, with the plan of exchanging the light-squared bishops. Once the Black king's bishop is exchanged for a knight this is particularly appropriate as it deprives White of the bishop pair. Here we see this strategy in action.

Game 24
Pytel-Plachetka
Zemun 1980

1	d4	♘f6
2	c4	e6
3	♘f3	♗b4+
4	♘bd2	0-0

Black delays committing himself in the centre, but he must take care to obtain counterplay.

| 5 | e3 | d5 |
| 6 | a3 | ♗xd2+ |

Black could retreat the bishop to e7, which would lead to a type of Queen's Gambit, but he has a different plan in mind.

| 7 | ♗xd2 | |

A good alternative would be to take with the queen and fianchetto the queen's bishop with b2-b3 and ♗b2.

| 7 | ... | b6 |
| 8 | ♗d3 | ♗a6 |

The point of Black's opening play; the pin of the pawn on c4 is unpleasant for White. He could defend with 9 b3, but then Black could continue with ...♘bd7 and ...c7-c5.

9   ♕e2   ♘bd7

Black does not exchange immediately on c4 to swap the bishops, as this would lead to White obtaining pressure down the half-open c-file after 9...dxc4 10 ♗xc4 ♗xc4 11 ♕xc4 followed by 12 ♖c1. Instead Black prepares to play ...c7-c5 when White cannot capture on c5 because of ...♘xc5.

10   0-0   c5

Black is now planning to exchange on d4, which would be awkward for White if he were to capture with the knight as the black knight could then come to e5 with effect; and if White recaptures with the pawn, Black can saddle him with an isolated pawn after ...dxc4. White therefore decides he must liquidate the centre pawns.

11   cxd5   ♗xd3

12   ♕xd3   exd5

Black recaptures with the pawn in order to obtain an outpost for his knight on e4.

13   dxc5   bxc5

Capturing with the knight is not so good, as it allows White an outpost on d4 for his knight.

Now Black has a pair of hanging pawns on d5 and c5, so White's strategy must be to put pressure on these pawns and to try and win one of them. However, in this position Black has sufficient counterplay, because he has a good outpost for his knight on e4 and pressure down the half-open b-file.

14   ♖ac1   ♕e7

It was better to play 14...♕b6, as this does not allow the white queen to invade later on a6.

15   ♗c3   ♖ac8

16   ♖fd1   ♖fd8

17   ♕f5 *(D)*

White slips up, allowing Black to seize the initiative. He could have obtained an advantage with 17 ♕a6 with an attack on Black's unprotected a-pawn.

17   ...   ♕e6

If White now exchanges queens then Black's centre is strengthened and he can commence active play on the queenside. Note that 18 ♕xe6 fxe6 19 ♘g5 is simply met by 19...♖e8 followed by 20...h6, driving away the knight.

18   ♕f4   h6

A very useful move; Black prevents the white knight coming to g5. The impetuous 18...♘e4 is well met by 19 ♘g5 ♘xg5 20 ♕xg5 when Black is in difficulties.

19   h3   ♘e4

Black's objective has been achieved; the knight occupies a fine outpost on e4. White realizes that he has lost the initiative and tries to simplify.

20   ♕g4   ♘xc3

21   ♖xc3

Now Black could exchange queens: 21...♕xg4 22 hxg4 ♘f6 23 g5 hxg5 24 ♘xg5, but this is satisfactory for White. Instead he gains another tempo by attacking the white queen.

21   ...   ♘f6

22   ♕xe6   fxe6

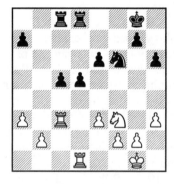

So the endgame has been reached and Black has a slight positional advantage. His big pawn centre controls many important squares and the pawn on e6 is very useful, since the d5 pawn is now securely protected, freeing the rook on d8 and knight on f6 for other activities.

23   ♘e5   ♘e4

24   ♖b3   ♖b8

25   ♖xb8   ♖xb8

26   f3   ♘f6

The alternative 26...♘d6 was bad because of 27 e4 d4 28 b4 cxb4 29 ♘c6 with good play for White.

27   ♖d2   ♖b3
28   ♔f2   ♔f8
29   ♖c2   ♔e7

White cannot capture on c5; 30 ♖xc5 ♖xb2+ 31 ♔g3 ♔d6 32 ♘d3 ♖b3 and wins.

30   ♔e2   c4

Black is planning to attack the white knight by ...♔d6 and then advance in the centre with ...e6-e5.

31   ♘c6+   ♔d6
32   ♘d4

32 ♘xa7 ♔c7 followed by 33...♔b7 wins the white knight.

32   ...   ♖b7

Black's plan is to play 33...e5 and after 34 ♘f5+ play 34...♔c5 and advance the d-pawn.

33   b4

A fine defensive move. If Black now captures en passant, White can regain the pawn and equalize: 33...cxb3 34 ♖b2 e5 35

♖xb3 ♖xb3 36 ♘xb3 and the entry of the black king is prevented.

33   ...   a5!

Black tries to obtain the c5 square for his king.

34   bxa5

White should have continued with 34 ♖b2 e5 35 ♘c2 when he is on the defensive, but it is difficult for Black to break through since he has no route in for his king.

34   ...   e5
35   a6   ♖b6
36   a7   ♖a6
37   ♘b5+   ♔c5
38   ♖b2   d4

Black has achieved his objective, but White has some counterplay because of his a-pawn. Black is threatening to play ...♘d5, so White's next is forced.

39   e4   ♘d7

39...♘h5 with the idea of 40...♘f4 was better.

40   ♖b4   ♘b6

40...g5 would have stopped White from obtaining counterplay with f4.

48 ♖b1 d2+ winning.

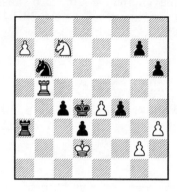

41   f4

The alternative 41 ♘c7 would reap dividends after 41...♖xa7 42 ♘e6+ ♚c6 43 ♘d8+ ♚c7 44 ♘e6+ ♚b7 45 ♘d8+ ♚b7 45 ♘d8+ ♚a6 with a satisfactory position for White. However, a better try for Black is 41...♖xa3 42 ♖xb6 ♚xb6 43 a8♕ ♖xa8 44 ♘xa8+ ♚b7 45 f4 ♚xa8 46 fxe5 ♚b7 winning.

| 41 | ... | exf4 |
| 42 | ♘c7 | |

The alternatives do not help White, e.g. 42 e5 ♘d7 or 42 ♘xd4 ♖xa3 43 ♘c2 ♖a2 44 ♚d1 ♖xa7 winning.

42	...	d3+
43	♚d2	♖xa3
44	♖b5+	♚d4 *(D)*

The most accurate move, since 44...♚c6 45 ♖xb6+ ♚xc7 46 ♖b4 leaves White some drawing chances. Now Black threatens ...c4-c3+ followed by ...♖a1+.

| 45 | ♘e6+ | ♚xe4 |
| 46 | ♘c5+ | |

Or 46 ♖xb6 c3+ 47 ♚c1 ♖a1+

| 46 | ... | ♚d5 |
| 47 | ♘a6+ | |

47 ♘xd3+ ♚c6 48 ♖c5+ ♚d6 wins for Black.

47	...	♚d4
48	♖xb6	c3+
49	♚e1	c2
50	♚d2	♖a1
51	♖b4+	♚e5
52	♖b5+	♚f6
53	♖b6+	♚g5
54	a8♕	c1♕+
55	♚xd3	♕e3+
56	♚c4	♖c1+
57	♚b5	♕b3+
58	♘b4	♕c4+
	0-1	

After 59 ♚a5 ♖a1+ 60 ♘a2 ♖xa2 is mate.

Bogo-Indian endings

Since some of the strategy of Black's opening play is directed at the endgame, it is worthwhile devoting a small section to this theme.

Game 25
Gulko-Muratov
USSR 1981

1	d4	♘f6
2	c4	e6
3	♘f3	♗b4+
4	♗d2	♕e7
5	g3	0-0
6	♗g2	♗xd2+

This allows White to set up his pieces favourably with his queen on d2 and knight on c3; if Black wishes to avoid this he must play ...♘c6 on move five.

7	♕xd2	d6
8	♘c3	e5
9	0-0	♘c6
10	d5	♘b8
11	e4	a5
12	♘e1	♘a6
13	♘d3	♘c5

Black has played slightly unusually, and his play is worth examining. If White now captures on c5 then after 14 ♘xc5 dxc5 Black will reposition his knight on the good square d6 via e8, so

Gulko decides to continue with his kingside play.

14	f4	♘xd3
15	♕xd3	♘d7
16	f5	♘c5

White has a big spatial advantage and possibilities of a kingside attack and it seems as though Black has no activity. However, the black structure is very solid and the exchange of two minor pieces has eased his task.

17	♕e3	f6

Black must prevent White from breaking up his kingside position with f6.

18	h4	♗d7
19	g4	g5

This must have come as a surprise to Gulko, as it seems that this move is unplayable.

20	hxg5	fxg5

Now it looks as though White can win immediately with 21 f6

because then 21...♖xf6 loses to 22 ♕xg5+. But with 21...♕f7 22 ♕xg5+ ♔h8 23 ♕h4 ♖g8 24 g5 ♖g6 25 ♖f3 h6 26 ♖g3 ♕h7 27 gxh6 ♖xg3 28 ♕xg3 ♕xh6 Black will round up the white pawns. Gulko contents himself instead with a quiet move, but Black is now able to consolidate.

21	♗f3	♕g7
22	♔g2	♖f6
23	♖h1	♗e8
24	b3	♖h6

Black continues his policy of exchanging pieces, confident of his endgame chances.

25	♖xh6	♕xh6
26	♗d1	♕g7
27	♘e2	♘d7
28	♘g1	♘f6
29	♘h3	h6

Black's knight on f6 is well placed, pressurizing both the e4 and g4 pawns.

30	♘f2	♕e7
31	a3	c6

This gives Black possibilities of exchanging on d5 or attempting to break up the white pawn

chain with ...b7-b5.

32	♗e2	♔g7

Black simply protects his h-pawn. Note that White cannot plunge in with 32 ♕b6 since 32...c5 and ...♖a6 traps the white queen.

33	dxc6	bxc6

White should have tried to retain the tension as now Black can use the half-open b-file. Although Black's d-pawn is slightly weak, White's b-pawn is more vulnerable and of greater significance.

34	♖d1	♕c7
35	♕c3	c5
36	b4	cxb4
37	axb4	♕b6

A drop of poison. Black threatens the combination ...♕xf2+, ...♘xe4+ and ...♘xc3 winning, so White is forced into a bad ending.

38	♕d3	♕xb4
39	♕xd6	♕xd6
40	♖xd6	a4

So the queens have been exchanged and Black has a big advantage because of his better minor piece and outside passed pawn. The white rook must now retreat in order to stop this pawn.

41 ♜d2 ♝c6

The black bishop triumphantly emerges; its white counterpart is languishing behind its own infantry.

42 ♛f3 ♕f7
43 ♛e3 ♕e7
44 ♝d1 ♜d8

Black exchanges rooks in order to advance his king via the queenside dark squares into the white position. White cannot move his rook off the d-file: 45 ♜a2 ♜d4 or 45 ♜c2 ♞xe4 46 ♞xe4 ♜xd1 are winning for Black.

45 ♜xd8 ♕xd8
46 ♕d3 ♕c7
47 ♕c3 a3
48 ♝c2 ♕d6

Now if White tries to capture the a-pawn he meets his doom with a tactical trick: 49 ♕b3 ♝a4+ and if 50 ♕xa4 a2 wins or 50 ♕c3 a2 51 ♕b2 ♝xc2 wins.

49 ♝b1 a2
50 ♝xa2 ♝xe4

This is much better than capturing with the knight as the knight on f6 blockades White's passed f-pawn. Now Black threatens ...♝f3 followed by ...♝xg4, so White exchanges the bishop.

51 ♞xe4+ ♞xe4
52 ♕b4 ♞f6
53 ♕b5 ♕c7

It is important to firmly blockade the c-pawn; bad would be 53...♞xg4, since then White could play 54 ♕b6 with the threat of c4-c5+.

54 ♕c5 h5

Fine endgame play. If White captures on h5, then after 55...g4 he cannot stop the g-pawn, while the black knight holds both of White's passed pawns on the kingside.

55 ♝b1 h4
56 ♝d3 h3
57 ♝e2 h2
58 ♝f3 e4
0-1

White resigned because after 59 ♝g2 e3 he cannot stop both of

Black's pawns.

Black must be very careful of endgames where White has the two bishops, as in Portisch-Andersson. Andersson was very fortunate to win the next game, as he was under great pressure for most of the time.

Game 26
Korchnoi-Andersson
Wijk aan Zee 1983

1	d4	♘f6
2	c4	e6
3	♘f3	♗b4+
4	♘bd2	b6
5	a3	♗xd2+
6	♗xd2	♗b7

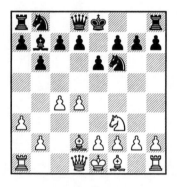

Now Korchnoi puts a new slant on the opening by repositioning his queen's bishop actively on the kingside.

| 7 | ♗g5 |

This is much better than 7 e3, blocking the queen's bishop behind the pawn chain; and after 7 g3 Black can play the interesting 7...♗xf3 8 exf3 ♘c6.

7	...	h6
8	♗h4	d6
9	e3	♘bd7

| 10 | ♗d3 | ♕e7 |

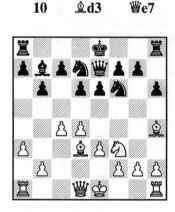

Andersson waits to see if White will incautiously castle kingside, as after 11 0-0 g5 12 ♗g3 h5 13 h4 gxh4 14 ♗xh4 ♖g8 15 e4 0-0-0 Black has strong play down the open g-file.

| 11 | b4 |

Korchnoi in turn plays a useful waiting move. If Andersson were to respond with 11...0-0-0 then Korchnoi could commence a pawn storm on the queenside with a4-a5. Andersson is understandably reluctant to play 11...g5, as this would weaken his kingside.

| 11 | ... | a5 |
| 12 | 0-0 | axb4 |

13	axb4	0-0

bishop on b7 is rather exposed to attacks by the white major pieces.

The game is already drifting towards an endgame in which White will hold a slight advantage because of his two bishops.

14 ♕e2

14 ♘d2 was best, controlling the important e4 square.

| 14 | ... | c5 |
| 15 | e4 | |

This move tempts Black to take a pawn by 15...g5 16 ♗g3 g4 17 ♘d2 cxd4 but after 18 f4 White has very good compensation for the pawn: Black's kingside is very weak; White has the immediate threat of 19 e5 and he can reintroduce a nasty pin with ♗h4 at some stage. Andersson decides to block the position.

15	...	e5
16	bxc5	bxc5
17	d5	

White stands better, as there is still a nagging pin on the knight on f6 and Black dare not drive the bishop away by ...g7-g5, since this would fatally weaken his kingside. Furthermore, the black

| 17 | ... | ♖fb8 |
| 18 | ♖fb1 | |

White threatens to play 19 ♖xa8 ♗xa8 20 ♖xb8 ♘xb8 21 ♕a2 ♗b7 22 ♕a7 ♕c7 23 ♗xf6 gxf6 24 ♘h4 followed by ♘f5 with a winning advantage.

18	...	♖xa1
19	♖xa1	♗c8
20	♖a7	♕d8
21	♕a2	♘f8

Black's plan is to play his knight to g6 at some point, driving away the annoying bishop.

| 22 | ♖a8 | ♖xa8 |

Andersson had a chance to gain some activity here by 22...♗g4 23 ♖xb8 ♕xb8; then after 24 ♗xf6 ♗xf3 25 ♗xe5 dxe5 26 gxf3 ♘g6 Black has good positional compensation for the pawn, so White should play 24 ♘d2, though after 24...g5 25 ♗g3 ♘g6 the black pieces are more active.

23	♕xa8	g5
24	♗g3	♕c7
25	h4	

25   ...   ♘6h7

White probes the black king-side. Timman analyses two variations after 25...g4: (a) 26 ♘h2 ♘h5 27 ♘f1 ♘f4 28 ♗c2 with the idea of ♘e3; and (b) 26 ♘h2 ♘g6 27 ♘f1 ♘f4 28 ♗xf4 exf4 29 e5 dxe5 30 ♗f5 ♘d7 31 d6 ♕d8 32 ♗xg4, each of which results in a clear advantage for White. In both cases the advance of the pawn to g4 only creates a weakness.

26   hxg5

Unnecessary; White should simply retreat his knight to e1, planning to move it to c2 and e3.

26	...	hxg5
27	♘e1	♗d7
28	♘c2	♕b6
29	♘e3	♘f6
30	♔h2	♔g7
31	♗c2 (D)	

White's plan is to play f2-f3 followed by ♗e1-a5. Andersson decides to exchange the strong white knight on e3 so that he can use his queen for counterplay.

31   ...   ♘g4+

32	♘xg4	♗xg4
33	♕e8	

Now Andersson could have obtained a draw by counterattacking with his queen: 33...♕b2 34 ♗a4 (not 34 ♕e7 ♕xc2 35 ♕xg5 + ♘g6 36 ♕xg4 ♕xc4 with advantage to Black) 34...♕e2 35 ♕e7 ♘g6 36 ♕xd6 ♕xe4 37 ♕xc5 ♘f4 38 ♘xf4 ♕xf4+ 39 ♔g1 (39 g3 ♕f5 with the idea of ...♗f3 and ...♕h7+ wins for Black) 39...♕c1+ 40 ♔h2 ♕f4+ with a draw by perpetual check.

33	...	♕c7
34	♗a4	♘h7

34...♗d7 loses immediately to 35 ♕e7.

35 f3 ♘f6

An improvement was 35...♗c8, stopping the white queen from going to a8 and keeping ...♘f6 in reserve.

36 ♕a8 ♗d7
37 ♗c6

Now Black dare not exchange on c6, giving White a strong c-pawn.

37 ... ♕c8
38 ♕a4 ♔f8
39 ♗e1 ♔e7
40 ♕a7

This pin is awkward for Black and it is hard to see what he can do. Timman analyses a possible defence 40...♕h8+ 41 ♔g1 g4 42 f4 (or 42 fxg4 ♕h6 with the threat of ...♕e3+ and perpetual check) 42 ...♕h5 43 fxe5 ♕xe5 44 ♗h4 ♕d4+ 45 ♔h2 ♕e5+ with a draw by perpetual check. Instead Andersson blunders.

40 ... ♘e8?

Now Korchnoi could have concluded the game with 41 ♗b7

♕d8 42 ♗a5 ♘c7 43 ♗c6 ♗xc6 44 dxc6 winning a piece.

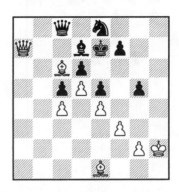

41 ♗a5? ♘f6
42 g4

Again Korchnoi misses a chance to press home his advantage with 42 ♗d2 ♘h7 43 g4 f6 44 ♗a5 ♘f8 45 ♗c7 threatening to move the queen to b6 and attack the weak d6 pawn, which cannot be defended by the black pieces.

42 ... ♔f8
43 ♗b7 ♕e8
44 ♕b6

The natural 44 ♗c7 is well met by 44...♔g7 45 ♗xd6 ♕h8+ and now (a) 46 ♔g2 ♗xg4 47 fxg4 ♘xg4 48 ♕xc5 ♕h2+ 49 ♔f3 ♕d2 50 ♔xg4 ♕g2+ 51 ♔f5 ♕f3+ 53 ♔xg5 ♕g3+ 53 ♔h5 ♕h3+ 54 ♔g5 f6 mate; or (b) 46 ♔g1 ♕h4 with a draw by perpetual check.

44 ... ♕b8
45 ♗d2 ♘h7
46 ♔g3 f6
47 ♗a5 ♔e7
48 ♕a6 ♘f8

So Andersson has escaped from his trial and is now threatening ...♘g6 followed by ...♛h8. Korchnoi, probably due to fatigue, slips up and exchanges queens; 49 ♔f2 ♘g6 50 ♔e3 ♘f4 51 ♛b6 ♛h8 52 ♗c6 was still good enough for a draw.

49	♛a8	♛xa8
50	♗xa8	

Now the weak black pawns on d6 and f6 are defended, but the white pawns on c4 and f3 are open to attack by the black bishop and black knight.

50	...	♗a4
51	♗c6	♗d1
52	♗d2	♘g6
53	♗e3	♘h4
54	f4	exf4+

55	♗xf4	gxf4+
56	♔xh4	♗c2
57	♔h3	♗xe4
58	♗a4	♔f7
59	♗d1	♗d3
	0-1	

After 60 ♗b3 ♔g6 61 ♔h4 f5 62 gxf5+ ♔xf5 63 ♔h3 ♔e4 64 ♔g2 ♔e3 his only way to stop the f-pawn is 65 ♗d1, when the c-pawn drops. This tremendous struggle underlines the long defensive task Black may be saddled with if he does not play actively in the 4 ♘bd2 line.

1 4 ♘c3

In this chapter we shall look at the positions arising from the sequence **1 d4 ♘f6 2 c4 e6 3 ♘f3 ♗b4+ 4 ♘c3**.

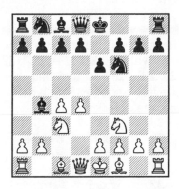

Strangely enough this move is not often seen in this move order, though this position is often reached via the Nimzo-Indian after 1 d4 ♘f6 2 c4 e6 3 ♘c3 ♗b4 4 ♘f3. Black normally now elects to fianchetto his queen's bishop with ...b7-b6, and we shall concentrate on this possibility; although Black can also stake an immediate claim in the centre with ...c7-c5, this leads to positions which are quite difficult for him to handle, as the following game show.

Game 27
Rubinstein-Maroczy
London 1922

1	d4	♘f6
2	♘f3	e6
3	c4	♗b4+
4	♘c3	

At the time this game was played, this move was unusual since theory had not yet decided whether Black could advantageously double White's pawns with 4...♗xc3+ 5 bxc3 d6.

4	...	c5
5	g3	♘e4
6	♗d2	♘xd2
7	♕xd2	♕a5
8	♗g2	0-0
9	0-0	cxd4
10	♘xd4 (D)	
10	...	♘c6

If Black exchanges on c3 then White can take a grip on the d6 square: 10...♗xc3 11 bxc3 ♘c6 12 ♘b5 when it is difficult for Black to develop his queen's bishop.

| 11 | ♖fc1 | ♕c5 |
| 12 | ♘xc6 | bxc6 |

Black hopes to build up a strong pawn centre with a later ...d7-d5, but he finds this impossible to achieve. Preferable was 12...dxc6 13 a3 ♗xc3 14 ♖xc3 e5 when the black bishop can emerge on e6.

13	a3	♗xc3
14	♖xc3	a5
15	b3	f5

Black wishes to prevent White from establishing a bind on the position. The black queen is badly tied to the c5 square since if it moves then White can play c4-c5, when Black has a terrible weakness on d7. 15...♖a7 was worth consideration.

| 16 | e4 | ♖b8 |

Again 16...♖a7 merits attention.

| 17 | a4 | fxe4 |

| 18 | ♗xe4 | ♖f7 |
| 19 | ♖e1 | ♗b7 |

If 19...♕b4 20 c5 holds Black in a vice.

| 20 | ♔g2 | ♖bf8 |
| 21 | f3 | g6 |

This weakens the kingside; 21...d6 was better.

22	♖d1	♗a8
23	h4	♗b7
24	♖dc1	d6
25	♖d1	♖d8
26	f4	♕b4

After 26...e5 27 f5 gxf5 28 ♕g5+ wins for White.

| 27 | ♖e3 | ♕b6 |

Black could have exchanged queens with 27...♕xd2+ 28 ♖xd2 d5 29 ♗f3 ♖e7 30 ♖e5, but then White has a good ending because of the weak black pawns.

28	♗f3	c5
29	♗xb7	♕xb7+
30	♔h2	♕e7
31	♖de1	♖f6
32	♕xa5	♖df8
33	♕d2	h6
34	♖1e2	♔h7
35	♕d5	1-0

Black has no counterplay and is still saddled with the weak e-pawn.

The German theoretician Sämisch was the first player to develop a viable system of counterplay with the fianchetto 4...b6, and it is this plan which is now the most popular.

Game 28
Marshall-Sämisch
Moscow 1925

1	d4	♘f6
2	♘f3	e6
3	c4	♗b4+
4	♘c3	b6
5	♕b3	♕e7
6	♗f4	

This move does not exert any influence on the central light squares; 6 ♗g5 was better.

6	...	♗xc3+
7	♕xc3	d6
8	e3	♗b7
9	♗d3	♘e4
10	♕c2	f5
11	h4	

A rather weakening move; White should consider 11 0-0-0 or 11 ♘d2.

11	...	♘d7
12	0-0-0	0-0-0
13	♖hg1	♔b8
14	♗f1	h6
15	♗d3	g5
16	♗g3	♘xg3
17	fxg3	gxh4
18	gxh4	

Black now has considerable pressure down the half-open g-file.

18	...	♘f6
19	♕a4	♖hg8
20	♗e2	♖g3
21	♖d3	♕d7

This careful move prevents White from generating a queen-side attack with ♖a3.

22	♕d1	♖dg8

23	♕f1	♕g7

A triumph for Black's strategy; White now loses his g-pawn without compensation. Marshall tries to complicate matters but this leads to further losses, and the rest of the game is rather painful for White who loses most of his pawns.

24	d5	♖xg2
25	♖xg2	♕xg2
26	♘d4	♕xf1+
27	♗xf1	exd5
28	cxd5	♗xd5
29	♖d1	♖g1
30	♘xf5	♗xa2
31	♔c2	♗e6
32	♘d4	♗d5
33	♗d3	♖xd1
34	♔xd1	a5
35	♔e2	♔c8
36	♘f5	♘g8
37	e4	♗e6
38	♘d4	♗d7
39	♔e3	♘f6
40	♔f4	♘h5+
41	♔f3	♔d8
42	♘c2	c6
43	♘e3	b5
44	♘c2	♔e7
45	♘d4	♔f6
46	♔e3	♘g7
47	♗e2	a4
48	♗f1	♘e8
49	♘f3	♘c7
50	♔f4	♘e6+
51	♔e3	♘c7

52	♔f4	c5
53	e5+	♔e7
54	h5	d5
55	♘h4	c4
56	♘f3	♘e6+
57	♔e3	b4
58	♔d2	♗e8
59	♘e1	♘d4
60	♘g2	♘f3+

61	♔c2	♗xh5
62	♘f4	♗f7
63	♗h3	♘xe5
64	♗g2	♔d6
0-1		

The following games show the modern treatment of White fighting for control of the centre with 5 ♗g5.

Game 29
Gheorghiu-Miles
London 1980

1	d4	♘f6
2	c4	e6
3	♘c3	♗b4
4	♘f3	b6
5	♗g5	

This system often features opposite castling, usually 0-0 for White and ...0-0-0 for Black, and attacks on opposite wings. Black must be careful when driving away the bishop with ...h7-h6 and ...g7-g5, since this weakens his kingside.

| 5 | ... | h6 |
| 6 | ♗h4 | g5 |

As noted above, this is a double-edged move. Black weakens his kingside, but fights for control of e4.

7	♗g3	♘e4
8	♕c2	♗b7
9	e3	♗xc3+

The risky 9...f5 is considered later in the game Keene-Burger.

| 10 | bxc3 | |

Black can now choose between two strategies: 10...d6 followed by 11...f5 to support his knight on its outpost on e4; or an exchange with 10...♘xg3 (or even 10...d6 11 ♗d3 ♘xg3, as in the game Torre-Spassky later in this chapter). The former strategy is fraught with danger as was shown by the miniature Ribli-Seirawan, Malta (Olympiad) 1980, which continued 10...d6 11 ♗d3 f5 12 d5 exd5 13 cxd5 ♗xd5 14 ♘d4 ♕f6 15 f3 ♘c5 16 ♗xf5 ♘bd7 17 ♘b5 0-0-0 18 ♖d1 ♗e6 19 ♗e4 ♔b8 20 ♖xd6 ♘e5 21 ♖xd8+ ♖xd8 22 0-0 ♗d7 23 ♘d4 ♗a4 24 ♗xe5 and Black resigned.

10 ... ♘xg3

The safest choice.

11 hxg3

White can also try 11 fxg3 with the idea of attacking down the half-open f-file. Play might continue 11...g4 12 ♘h4 ♕g5 13 ♕d2 ♘c6 14 ♗d3 f5 15 0-0, when White stands slightly better, as in Salov-Timman, Brussels 1988.

11 ... ♘c6

The main alternative 11...♕e7 is considered in the next game, Karpov-Speelman. Also possible is 11...g4 12 ♘e5 ♕g5 13 ♖h4 f5 14 c5 ♘c6 15 ♘d3 with a slight advantage to White.

12 ♖b1

White plans to use the half-open b-file to attack Black's queenside by the thrusts c5 and a5. Instead Pinter-Chandler, Hastings 1980/81, went 12 ♘d2 ♕e7 13 ♘b3 ♕a3 stopping the white queenside advance and giving Black a good game. In-

stead of 13 ♘b3, 13 a4 ♘a5 14 ♘b3 ♘xb3 15 ♕xb3 c5 16 a5 ♕d6 is also satisfactory for Black. Modern theory recommends 12 ♖h5 ♕f6 13 g4 ♘e7 14 ♘d2 c5 15 g3 with a slight pull for White, as in Ionescu-Kengis, Timisoara 1987.

12 ... ♕e7
13 c5 h5

Black's strategy is clear; he will open the diagonal of his bishop by ♘a5 and then open up the kingside with a combination of ...g5-g4 and ...h5-h4.

14 ♗e2

After 14 g4 0-0-0 15 gxh5 g4 16 ♘d2 f5 Black will eventually round up the h-pawn with a good game.

14 ... ♘a5
15 ♘d2 ♗xg2
16 ♖xh5 0-0-0

Black now has good chances, since he can penetrate down the open h-file. White has counterchances on the queenside, but Miles defends carefully.

17 cxb6 axb6

18	♖xh8	♖xh8
19	♗f3	♗xf3
20	♘xf3	♕f6
21	♔e2	♘c4
22	♕a4	d5!

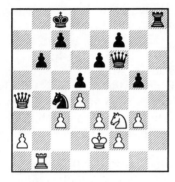

Black now has a big positional advantage because of his strong knight on c4 and the shaky position of the white knight on f3. White now achieves nothing by 23 ♕a8+ ♔d7 24 ♕a4+ ♔e7 25 ♕b4+ ♔d8 so he decides to take a pawn instead.

23	♘xg5	♔b7!
24	♘f3	♕f5

25	♖c1	♕g4

Black now threatens to win the pinned knight by ... ♖h5-f5.

26	♕d1	♖h5
27	♔f1	♖h1+
28	♘g1	

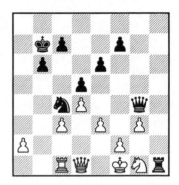

28	...	♘xe3+
29	fxe3	♕xg3
30	♔e2	♖h2+
	0-1	

It is mate after 31 ♔d3 ♕g6+. A fine game and a good model for Black's general strategy in this opening variation.

Game 30
Karpov-Speelman
London 1982

1	d4	♘f6
2	c4	e6
3	♘f3	b6
4	♘c3	♗b4
5	♗g5	h6
6	♗h4	♗b7
7	e3	g5
8	♗g3	♘e4

9	♕c2	♗xc3+
10	bxc3	♘xg3
11	hxg3	♕e7
12	♗d3	

Plaskett-Hebden, England 1982, saw instead 12 a4 ♘c6 13 ♘d2 ♘a5 14 ♘b3 ♘xb3 15 ♕xb3 ♕f6 16 a5 0-0 17 ♖h2 c5 18 ♗d3 d5 with dynamic equality.

12	...	♘c6
13	♖b1	

13 ♖h5 is perhaps more accurate.

| 13 | ... | 0-0-0 |

A bold decision; Speelman castles into White's attack since he is well positioned to beat it off.

14	c5	d6
15	cxb6	cxb6

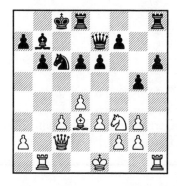

The position is slightly better for Black because of his superior development and the isolation of White's king's rook.

16	c4	♔b8
17	♘d2	

Karpov plays this knight away from the kingside, but it is hard to see a safe alternative.

17	...	h5
18	♕a4	h4
19	gxh4	gxh4
20	♖b5	f5

The white g-pawn is very vulnerable now, so Karpov repositions his bishop only to meet up with a neat combination.

21	♗e2	♕g7
22	♗f3	e5
23	d5	e4
24	dxc6	exf3

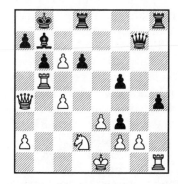

The point of Black's combination is seen clearly after 25 cxb7 fxg2 26 ♖g1 h3 when the black h-pawn is a winner. In addition 25 ♘xf3 ♕xg2 26 ♖g1 ♕xf3 27 c7+ ♔xc7 28 ♕xa7 ♕c6 29 ♖xb6 ♕xb6 30 ♖g7+ ♔c6 31 ♕a4+ ♔c5 leaves White with no useful checks.

25	gxf3	♗xc6
26	♖xb6+	axb6
27	♕xc6	♕c7

28   ♕a4

After the fireworks Black has emerged the exchange to the good; he could now continue with 28...h3, which would have made it very hard for White to survive more than a few moves.

28   ...   d5?
29   c5   ♕xc5

29 ... bxc5 is a good try since after 30 ♖xh4 ♖xh4 31 ♕xh4 the black c-pawn can be used to tie down the white pieces by 31...c4.

30   ♖xh4   ♖xh4
31   ♕xh4   ♖g8
32   a4

The only move to prevent 32...♖g1+ followed by 33...♕b5+.

32   ...   ♕a5
33   ♔d1   ♖g1+
34   ♔c2   ♕c5+
35   ♔d3   ♖c1

36   ♔e2

Here White should have played 36 ♕d8+ ♔a7 37 ♕d7+ ♔a6 38 ♕d8 when it is hard for Black to make progress.

36   ...   ♕c8!
37   f4   ♕a6+?

A great pity, as now the white monarch flees to safety via f3. 37...♖c2, pinning the white knight, leaves White defenceless.

38   ♔f3   ♕xa4
39   ♕d8+   ♔a7
40   ♔g2   ♕c6
41   ♘f3   ♔a6
42   ♕f8   d4
43   ♕xf5   dxe3
44   fxe3   ♕c2+
45   ♕xc2   ♖xc2+
46   ♔g3   ♖e2

This leads to a draw, since the white f-pawn advances and ties down the black rook. 46...♔b7, to stop the pawns with the king, was worth considering.

47   f5   ♖xe3
48   ♔f4   ♖e8
49   f6   ♔b5
50   f7   ♖f8
51   ♘e5   ♔b4
52   ♔f5   b5
53   ♔e6   ♔c3
54   ♘c6   ½-½

A tragedy for Speelman after his fine play in the middlegame.

Game 31
Torre-Spassky
Hamburg 1982

---

1   d4   ♘f6   2   ♘f3   b6

Again the opening sequence is different from the topic of the book, the Bogo-Indian, but such transpositions are worth knowing.

3	c4	e6
4	♘c3	♗b4
5	♗g5	h6
6	♗h4	♗b7
7	e3	g5
8	♗g3	♘e4
9	♕c2	♗xc3+
10	bxc3	d6
11	♗d3	♘xg3
12	hxg3	

White has the option of recapturing with the other pawn here. Timman-Miles, Tilburg 1985, continued 12 fxg3 ♘d7 13 0-0 ♕e7 14 ♖f2 0-0-0 15 ♗e4 f5 16 ♗xb7+ ♔xb7 17 e4 with a slight advantage to White.

| 12 | ... | ♘d7 |

A slightly different system to those we have seen before; Black develops his queen's knight on d7, preparing to transfer it to f6 where it will exert pressure on e4.

| 13 | a4 | |

13 ♗e4 immediately is perhaps more accurate.

| 13 | ... | a5 |

The prophylactic 13...♔e7 may be better here, intending to meet 14 a5 with 14...c5.

| 14 | ♗e4! | |

A good move from Torre; the exchange of light-squared bishops leaves Black weak on the queenside light squares.

| 14 | ... | ♗xe4 |
| 15 | ♕xe4 | ♔e7! |

A strange king move. After 15...♘f6 Black's king would be displaced by 16 ♕c6+ in any case, so Spassky moves the king first, reversing the order of moves.

16	♕c6	♘f6
17	♘d2	♕d7
18	♕b5	

In order to make any progress Black must exchange the white queen, but what then? He has a long-term weakness: the h-pawn on a half-open file. Spassky's handling of this difficult position is exemplary.

18	...	♕xb5
19	cxb5	♖ac8

Spassky plans to open the c-file by ...c7-c6 and then play against White's c-pawn.

20	♔e2	c5
21	bxc6	♖xc6
22	♖a3	

22 c4 is well met by 22...d5 when exchanging gives the black knight a fine post on d5.

22   ...   ♖hc8

Black gives up his h-pawn, apparently for nothing, since 23 ♖xh6 ♖xc3 24 ♖xc3 ♖xc3 25 ♖xf6 ♔xf6 26 ♘e4+ ♔e7 27 ♘xc3 wins for White. However, this is actually a fine positional pawn sacrifice.

23	♖xh6	d5!
24	♘b1	

24 ♔d3 ♘g4 is crushing.

24	...	♘e4
25	♖b3	g4!!

The key to Black's play; after the immediate 25...♘xc3+ 26 ♘xc3 ♖xc3 27 ♖xb6 ♖c2+ 28 ♔f3 White has a satisfactory game, but now Black plans

26...♘xc3+ 27 ♘xc3 ♖xc3 28 ♖xb6 ♖c2+ when the white king is badly tied down.

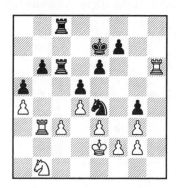

26	♖h7	♔f6
27	♖h6+	♔e7
28	♖h7	♖8c7

Spassky protects his second rank against a later ♖b7+ and now White must decide what to do about his c-pawn. Torre decides to jettison his f-pawn in order to save his c-pawn.

29	♔d3	♘xf2+
30	♔c2	♘e4
31	♖g7	♘xg3
32	♖xg4	♘e4

Material is equal, but White has weak pawns on g2, e3, c3 and a4, whereas Black has only one weakness on b6.

33	♖g8	♖c4
34	♖a3	♖c8
35	♖xc8	♖xc8
36	♖b3	♖g8 (D)

The black rook switches to the kingside to commence the final onslaught.

37	♖xb6	♖xg2+
38	♔b3	♖e2

39	**♖b5**	**♘d6**
40	**♖xa5**	**♘c4**
41	**♖a7+**	**♔f6**

White now has no defence to ... ♖b2+.

42	**a5**	**♖b2+**
43	**♔a4**	**♖xb1**
44	**a6**	**♘xe3**
45	**♖b7**	**♖a1+**
46	**♔b5**	**♘c4**
47	**♖d7**	**♖a5+**
	0-1	

A fine positional game by Spassky.

Black can also play aggressively by advancing his kingside pawns in this line, but this is risky, as the next game demonstrates.

Game 32
Keene-Burger
New York 1981

1	**d4**	**♘f6**
2	**♘f3**	**e6**
3	**♗g5**	**h6**
4	**♗h4**	**b6**
5	**e3**	**♗b7**
6	**c4**	**♗b4+**
7	**♘c3** *(D)*	

After an unusual opening sequence we have reached the basic position of this variation.

7	**...**	**g5**
8	**♗g3**	**♘e4**
9	**♕c2**	

It is worth considering the interesting sacrificial line 9 ♘d2 ♘xc3 10 bxc3 ♗xc3 11 h4 (11 ♖c1 ♗b4 12 h4 gxh4 13 ♖xh4 is also interesting) 11...♗xa1 12 ♕xa1 d5 13 hxg5 ♕xg5 14 cxd5 ♗xd5 15 ♗xc7 when White has good positional compensation for the exchange: the black kingside is wrecked, and it is difficult for the black king to find a safe haven.

9   ...   f5

This is more risky than exchanging on c3 and then on g3, since it leads to further weaknesses on the kingside.

10   ♗d3   ♗xc3+
11   bxc3   ♘xg3

This is clearly inappropriate here; Black should continue with 11...d6, planning to reinforce his control of e4 by ...♘d7-f6. Razuvayev-Salov, Moscow 1986, continued 12 d5 ♘d7! 13 ♗xe4 fxe4 14 ♕xe4 ♕f6 15 0-0 0-0-0 16 ♕e6 ♕xe6 17 dxe6 ♖de8 with an unclear endgame.

12   hxg3   ♘c6
13   d5   ♘a5

Now White rips open the black kingside.

14   g4!

This ensures the breakthrough of the white pieces on the kingside.

14   ...   fxg4?

This opens the black king to the fury of the white pieces;

14...♕f6 was much better, planning to escape with the king to the queenside.

15   ♗g6+   ♔e7
16   ♘e5   ♕g8
17   ♗h5

This excellent move plans to harass the black king further by ♘g6+.

17   ...   exd5

17...♕h7 is met by 18 ♕a4.

18   ♘g6+   ♔d6

18...♔d8 19 ♘xh8 ♕xh8 20 cxd5 ♗xd5 21 ♗xg4 ♗xg2 22 0-0-0 ♗c6 23 ♖xd7+ ♗xd7 24 ♖d1 ♔c8 25 ♖xd7 ♔b8 26 ♕d3 ♘b7 27 ♗f3 is terrible for Black.

19   ♘xh8   ♕xh8
20   cxd5   ♗xd5
21   ♖d1

White threatens 22 c4, winning a piece.

21   ...   ♔c5
22   ♗xg4   ♗xg2
23   ♗xd7

Now if Black captures the rook he is mated by 23...♗xh1 24 ♕f5+ ♔c4 25 ♕d3+ ♔c5 26 ♕b5+. Black should have tried 23...c6 here, but blunders instead, bringing the game to an abrupt conclusion.

23   ...   ♘c4
24   ♕b3   1-0

The following exciting game, in which Black slightly postpones his assault on the white queen's bishop, further illustrates the complexities of this variation.

Game 33
Kasparov-Karpov
World Championship (Game 18) 1986

1	d4	♘f6
2	c4	e6
3	♘f3	b6
4	♘c3	♗b4
5	♗g5	♗b7
6	e3	h6
7	♗h4	♗xc3+
8	bxc3	d6
9	♘d2	

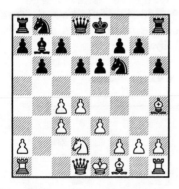

9	...	g5
10	♗g3	♕e7

Perhaps a better choice for Black is 10...♘bd7 11 h4 ♔e7!? 12 ♖b1 ♘e4 13 ♘xe4 ♗xe4 14 ♖b2 ♕g8 15 hxg5 hxg5 16 ♖xh8 ♕xh8 17 ♕g4 ♘f6 18 ♕xg5 ♖g8 19 ♕h4 ♕xh4 20 ♗xh4 ♗xg2 21 f3 ♗xf1 22 ♔xf1 ♖g6 23 ♖g2 ♖h6 24 ♗g5 ♖g6 when a draw was agreed in Ftacnik-Short, Dubai (Olympiad) 1986.

11	a4	a5

This is rather committal;

11...♘c6 with the idea of ...♘a5 was preferable.

12	h4	♖g8
13	hxg5	hxg5
14	♕b3	♘a6

Clearly 14...♘bd7 15 c5 dxc5 16 ♗xc7 is favourable for White.

15	♖b1	♔f8

If 15...0-0-0 16 c5 dxc5 17 ♘c4 White has a strong attack against the black king, so Karpov elects to move his king the other way.

16	♕d1	♗c6
17	♖h2	♔g7

Better was 17...♕d7, attacking the a-pawn and freeing the e7 square for the king is better; after 18 ♗d3 ♔e7 19 ♕e2 ♖h8 Black has counterplay.

18	c5	bxc5

After 18...dxc5 19 ♗e5 ♔f8 20 ♗b5 ♗b7 21 ♖h6 ♘d5 22 c4 ♘c3 23 ♕h5 ♘xb1 24 ♗f6 ♕d6

25 ♖h8 White wins.

19	♗b5	♘b8
20	dxc5	d5
21	♗e5	♔f8
22	♖h6	♘e8
23	♕h5	f6
24	♖h7	♘g7
25	♕f3	♔f7
26	♕h5+	♔f8
27	♕f3	♔f7
28	♖h6	

White could have taken a draw by perpetual check here.

28	...	♘e8
29	e4	

29 c4 g4 30 ♖h7+ ♖g7 31 ♖xg7+ ♘xg7 32 ♕f4 ♗xb5 33 ♖xb5 gives White the advantage.

29	...	g4
30	♕f4	♗xb5
31	♖xb5	♘d7
32	♗xc7	♘xc5

Better was 32...e5 33 ♕f5 ♘xc7 34 ♕h5+ ♔f8 35 ♖h7 ♖g7 36 ♖h8+ ♖g8 37 ♖h7 with a draw.

33	♕e3	♘xe4
34	♘xe4	dxe4
35	♗xa5	f5
36	♗b4	♕d7
37	♕d4	♖a7

37...♕xd4 38 ♖b7+ is good for White.

38	♖h7+	

Here 38 ♗c5 ♕xd4 39 ♗xd4 ♖c7 40 a5 is much better for White.

38	...	♘g7 (D)
39	a5	

Again 39 ♗c5 is good for White

39	...	♔g6

Also good for Black is 39...♕xb5 40 ♕xa7+ ♔g6 41 ♖h2 ♖d8 42 ♕e3 ♕a4 43 ♕c1 when the white pieces are badly tied down.

40	♕xd7	♖xd7
41	♖h4	

41	...	♖gd8
42	c4	♖d1+
43	♔e2	♖c1
44	a6	♖c2+
45	♔e1	♖a2
46	♖b6	♖d3
47	c5	♖a1+
48	♔e2	♖a2+
49	♔e1	g3

50	fxg3	♖xg3
51	♔f1	♖gxg2
52	♗e1	♖gc2
53	c6	♖a1
54	♖h3	f4
55	♖b4	♔f5

55...♘f5 56 ♖xe4 ♘g3+ 57 ♖xg3+ fxg3 58 ♖xe6+ ♔f7 59 ♖e3 g2+ should win for Black.

56	♖b5+	e5
57	♖a5	♖d1

More accurate is 57...♖ac1 58 c7 e3 59 ♖h2 ♖xh2 winning.

58	a7	

58 c7 e3 59 ♖h2 ♖xh2 60 c8(♕)+ ♘e6 wins for Black but White has a better move in 59 ♖a2 when Black is in great difficulty. Black should therefore play 58...♖cc1 59 a7 ♖xe1+ 60 ♔f2 e3+ 61 ♖xe3 fxe3+ 62 ♔f3 ♘e6 63 a8(♕) ♘g5+ 64 ♔g3 ♘e4+ winning.

58	...	e3
	0-1	

White has no defence to the threat of ...♖f2+ and ...♖xe1 mate.

In conclusion, 4 ♘c3 is a difficult line for Black to meet. It is best to concentrate on finding a safe haven for the king, e.g. castling queenside as in Karpov-Speelman, rather than go pawn-hunting.

2 4 ♘bd2 b6

Of White's various possible interpositions, 4 ♘bd2 is perhaps the sharpest line against the Bogo-Indian; White avoids the exchange of dark-squared bishops and this keeps the tension in the position. White aims to gain control of the e4 square in order to advance himself with e2-e4 in the centre. Black must decide how to combat this: he can build his own pawn centre with ...d7-d6 and ...e6-e5 (see Chapter 3), or play ...d7-d5 (see Chapter 4), but in this chapter we shall examine the most popular black strategy; to develop his queen's bishop by ...b7-b6. Black's aim by developing his bishop on b7 is to control the central light squares, especially e4. We have already seen some examples of this strategy in the introductory chapters, but here we systematically consider White's possible responses: 5 e3 (Games 34-36), 5 g3 (Game 37) and 5 a3 (Games 38-41).

Game 34
Lputian-Psakhis
USSR 1979

1	d4	♘f6
2	c4	e6
3	♘f3	♗b4+
4	♘bd2 *(D)*	
4	...	b6
5	e3	

The alternatives for White are 5 g3 or 5 a3, both of which are considered later in this chapter. The move played prepares to develop the king's bishop on d3, controlling the e4 square.

| 5 | ... | ♗b7 |

The immediate 5...c5 was considered in the game Portisch-Andersson in the Positional Themes chapter.

6   ♗d3   c5

Black stakes a claim in the centre. By playing ...c7-c5 Black has the option at a later stage of exchanging on d4 and/or playing ...d7-d5. The alternative 6...0-0 7 0-0 d5 was considered in the game Lputian-Petursson in the Historical Introduction.

7   0-0

The immediate 7 a3, forcing the exchange of the black bishop, is considered in the next game.

7   ...   cxd4

Perhaps 7...d5 is more accurate; after 8 dxc5 ♗xc5 9 a3 a5 10 b3 ♘c6 11 ♗b2 d5 Black has a fully equal position, as in Gheorghiu-Larsen, Las Palmas 1972.

8   exd4

If White recaptures with the knight then Black has good play: he can use the half-open c-file and post his knights on the c5 and e5 squares.

8   ...   0-0
9   a3   ♗e7

Black can also consider exchanging on d2 but then White might be able to create problems with ♗g5 with an awkward pin.

Black is behind in development due to moving his king's bishop twice, but this is not a major disadvantage in this position. White's knight on d2 is inactive and blocks the development of his queen's bishop, so White must spend time unravelling his queenside.

10   ♖e1   d5

Now Black's plan has become clear; he will exchange on c4 leaving White with an isolated pawn on d4.

11   cxd5   ♘xd5
12   ♘e4   ♘c6
13   ♗d2   ♖c8

Black has a positional advantage, since White has few attacking chances on the kingside. Black's intends to exchange pieces and eventually win the weak d-pawn.

14   ♖c1   ♘f6
15   ♗c3   ♘a5 *(D)*

Black prepares to exchange pieces on e4. White could exchange on a5, but the black a-pawns are not weak and Black has a good square on b6 for his queen.

16   ♕e2   ♘d5

With the threat of 17...♘f4, which White cannot allow.

17   ♗d2   ♖xc1

18   ♗xc1

18 ♖xc1 is worse because of 18...♘b3.

18	...	♘b3
19	♗e3	♘f6

White's d-pawn is under pressure already.

20   ♘xf6+   ♗xf6

White cannot now play 21 ♗xh7+ ♚xh7 22 ♕c2+ ♚g8 23 ♕xb3 ♗xf3 24 gxf3 ♗xd4 25 ♖d1 e5 because his shattered king position leaves Black clearly better.

21	♕c2	♗xf3
22	♕xb3	

22 ♗xh7+ ♚h8 23 ♕xb3 ♗d5 24 ♕c2 g6 25 ♗xg6 fxg6 26 ♕xg6 ♕d7 27 ♕h6+ ♚g8 wins for Black

22	...	♗b7

Now Black can play to win the white d-pawn.

23	♕c2	g6
24	♗e4	♕a8
25	f3	♖c8
26	♕d3	♖d8
27	♖c1	♖d7

At the moment White is defending satisfactorily, but in the long run he is doomed.

28	♖e1	♚g7
29	h3	♗d5
30	♖e2	♕d8
31	♖d2	

All the black pieces are trained on the weak d-pawn, but White can defend in equal force, so Black must find another weakness to attack.

31	...	♚g8
32	♗xd5	

Black was threatening 32...

♗xe4 33 fxe4 ♗xd4 34 ♗xd4 e5.

| 32 | ... | ♖xd5 |
| 33 | ♕e4 | ♗g7 |

Now Black is again threatening to win the d-pawn by ...e6-e5, which he could not do with the bishop on f6. This threat forces White to further weaken his position.

34	f4	h5
35	g3	♕d7
36	♔g2	♔h7
37	♔h2	a5

Black's pawn will advance to a4, creating an outpost on b3.

38	♔g2	a4
39	♔h2	♖b5
40	♔g2	♖b3
41	♗f2	♕b5

Now it is very difficult to defend his position: if 42 ♕c2 h4 43 gxh4 ♕d5+ wins; and 42 ♕b1 is impossible because of 42...♖xa3 and 42 ♕e2 ♕xe2 43 ♖xe2 ♖d3 wins the d-pawn.

| 42 | d5 | exd5 |
| 43 | ♖xd5 | f5 |

Now on 44 ♕e6, 44...♕c4 45 ♗d4 ♕c2+ 46 ♔h1 ♖xg3 and White is helpless.

44	♖xb5	fxe4
45	♖xb6	♖xb2
46	♖xb2	♗xb2
47	♗c5	

Material is still level, but Black has a won endgame since White's bishop is tied down to the a3 pawn and the white king must watch the passed e-pawn.

| 47 | ... | ♗c1 |
| 48 | ♔f2 | h4 |

Smashing the white pawn structure.

49	gxh4	♔g8
50	h5	gxh5
51	f5	♔f7
52	♗d4	♗xa3
53	♔e3	♗c1+

Black threatens ....♗b2 winning.

54	♔xe4	a3
55	♔d3	♗g5
56	♔c2	♗f6
57	♗c3	♗xc3
	0-1	

After 58 ♔xc3 ♔f6 59 ♔b3 ♔xf5 60 ♔xa3 h4 61 ♔b2 ♔f4 62 ♔c2 ♔g3 63 ♔d2 ♔xh3 64 ♔e2 ♔g2 wins.

In this game White played too passively in the opening and Black obtained easy equality. In the next two games we see a more aggressive plan of forcing Black to exchange on d2 and thus gaining the two bishops. Black must then be very careful.

Game 35
Miles-Andersson
Niksic 1983

1	d4	♘f6
2	c4	e6
3	♘f3	♗b4+
4	♘bd2	b6
5	e3	♗b7
6	♗d3	c5
7	a3	♗xd2+
8	♗xd2	d6

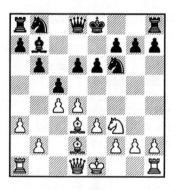

Black maintains a firm grip on the dark squares while preparing to develop his queen's knight on d7. The main alternative is 8...cxd4 9 exd4 d5.

9   dxc5

White can also keep the tension with 9 0-0 (see the next game).

9   ...   bxc5

This recapture retains control of e5; 9...dxc5 10 ♗c3 gives White a definite plus because of his two bishops, and control of e5.

10   0-0   a5

Black threatens to fix a hole in the white queenside by ...a5-a4, so Miles prevents this.

11   b3   ♘bd7

11 b4 is more active.

12	♕c2	♕c7
13	♗c3	

Miles is preparing 14 ♘d2, so Andersson decides to exchange off his bishop in order to wreck White's kingside.

13	...	♗xf3
14	gxf3	♘e5
15	♗xe5	

15 ♗e2 ♕c6 16 ♔g2 g5 is awkward for White since Black threatens to open the g-file with ...g5-g4.

15	...	dxe5
16	b4	♔e7

Black's king is safe here, and this is an important factor in any endgame. By placing his king on e7 Black also retains an option of a kingside pawn storm with ...g7-g5.

17	bxc5	♖ab8
18	♖fb1	♕xc5
19	♗e2	

It is hard to see what White should do.

19	...	♖hc8
20	♔f1	g5
21	♕a4	e4
22	♔g2	exf3+
23	♗xf3	g4
24	♗e2	

Black has dissolved his doubled pawn and can now take the initiative.

24	...	♘e4
25	♖b5	♖xb5
26	♕xb5	f5
27	♗d3	♘d6
28	♕b2	

If White exchanges queens then his pawns on the queenside become very weak.

28	...	♘f7
29	♖b1	♘e5
30	♗e2	h5

Black threatens to advance this pawn to h3 and create a mating net.

31	h3	♔f7
32	hxg4	hxg4
33	♕b5	♔e7
34	♖h1	♕xb5
35	cxb5	

In this endgame Black has the advantage because his knight is much better than the severely restricted bishop. White's passed pawn can easily be stopped and the white a-pawn is very weak.

35	...	♖c2
36	♖h7+	♔d6
37	♗f1	

White cannot sacrifice his

bishop; after 37 b6 ♖xe2 38 b7 ♘c6 the pawn is stopped.

37	...	♘d7
38	♖h8	♖a2
39	♖a8	♖xa3

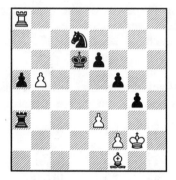

Black has made his first material gain and White is still hampered by his king being stuck on the kingside.

| 40 | ♖a6+ | ♔d5 |

White cannot push his pawn with 41 b6 because of 41...♔c6.

41	♖a8	♘b6
42	♖d8+	♔c5
43	♖e8	♔d6
44	♖d8+	♔c7

45	♖e8	♔d6
46	♖d8+	♔c7
47	♖e8	♖c3

Black has calculated that his a-pawn will win the game and he can afford to jettison the e-pawn.

48	♖xe6	a4
49	♖e7+	♔b8
50	♖e6	♔b7
51	♖e7+	♔b8

Black gains time by repeating the position since White has no alternative but to keep checking.

52	♖e6	♔b7
53	♖e7+	♖c7
54	♖xc7+	♔xc7
55	♗d3	a3
56	♗b1	♘d5
57	♗a2	♘c3
58	♗e6	♘xb5
59	e4	

59 ♔g3 ♔d6 60 ♗a2 ♔e5 followed by ...♘c3 also wins for Black.

| 59 | ... | f4 |
| **0-1** | | |

In the next game White maintains the tension in the centre.

Game 36
Smyslov-Kosten
Hastings 1988/89

1	d4	♘f6
2	♘f3	e6
3	c4	♗b4+
4	♘bd2	b6
5	e3	♗b7
6	♗d3	c5
7	a3	♗xd2+

8	♗xd2 *(D)*	
8	...	d6
9	0-0	♘bd7
10	♗c3	0-0
11	b4	

11 ♕e2 ♖c8 provides counter-play against the white c-pawn.

11	...	♕e7
12	♖e1	♗e4
13	♗f1	♖ac8
14	♘d2	♗b7
15	e4	cxd4
16	♗xd4	e5
17	♗b2	♖c7

An unclear position has arisen in which both sides have chances.

18	f3	♕e6
19	♖c1	♖fc8
20	♕b3	♘h5
21	♕e3	♘f4
22	g3	♕g6
23	♔h1	♘e6
24	♕d3	♘f6
25	♗g2	

Not now 25 ♕xd6 on account of 25...♖d8 winning.

25	...	h5
26	♘f1	♖d8
27	h4	

White could have tried 27 ♕e3 h4 28 ♕f2 removing his queen from the centre as Black is now able to open up the position to his advantage.

27	...	b5
28	cxb5	♖xc1
29	♖xc1	d5
30	♕e3	dxe4
31	fxe4	♗xe4
32	♗xe4	♘xe4
33	♖e1	f5
34	♗xe5	♖d3
35	♕xa7	

Not 35 ♕xd3 ♘f2+.

35	...	♕g4
36	♕g1	♖d5
37	♗a1	

Instead 37 ♘e3 ♕h3+ 38 ♕h2 ♘f2+ 39 ♔g1 ♕xh2+ 40 ♔xh2 ♖xe5 41 b6 ♘d8 is not an easy position for Black to win, whereas he can now continue his attack against the white king.

37	...	♘f4
38	♕h2	

After 38 gxf4 ♕xh4+ 39 ♘h2 ♘g3+ 40 ♔g2 ♖d2+ 41 ♔f3 ♖xh2 42 ♕xg3 ♖h3 43 ♖g1 ♖xg3+ 44 ♖xg3 ♕h1+ 45 ♔e3 ♕xa1 wins.

38	...	♕f3+
39	♔g1	♘h3+

40	♕xh3	♕f2+
41	♔h1	♕xe1
	0-1	

In conclusion, Black seems to have excellent chances in the 5 e3

system.

Instead of 5 e3 and 6 ♗d3, White sometimes chooses to fianchetto his king's bishop, leading to positions reminiscent of the main line Queen's Indian.

Game 37
Karpov-Andersson
Madrid 1973

1	d4	♘f6
2	c4	e6
3	♘f3	♗b4+
4	♘bd2	b6
5	g3	♗b7
6	♗g2	

The opening has transposed to a Bogo-Indian from a Queen's Indian.

6	...	0-0
7	0-0	c5

It is probably better to preserve the bishop with 7...d5 and if 8 a3 ♗e7.

8	a3	♗xd2
9	♗xd2	

White has the two bishops, but Black has a satisfactory position. He should now consider either 9 ...d6 or 9...d5. Andersson plays a seemingly natural move, but one that allows the white bishop to spring into action.

9	...	cxd4
10	♗b4	♖e8

10...d6 11 ♕xd4 is good for White.

11	♗d6	♘e4

11...♗xf3 12 ♗xf3 ♘c6 13 ♗xc6 dxc6 14 ♕xd4 may be a better alternative for Black.

12	♕xd4	♘a6
13	b4	♖c8

14	♖ac1

Black is tied down by the white bishop on d6 and must always be prepared to defend the pawn on d7 if White moves the bishop.

14	...	♘xd6
15	♕xd6	♘c7
16	♖fd1	♖e7
17	♕d3	

White now has the threat of 18 ♘g5 winning. 17...♖e8 loses the d-pawn and White can still play ♘g5 after 17 ...h6. 17 ...g6 18 ♘e5 is also very awkward for Black because of the possibility of ♘c6, so Andersson decides to give up his bishop.

17	...	♗xf3

17...d5 18 e4 is very awkward for Black.

18	♗xf3	♘e8
19	♗b7	

This move upsets the co-ordination of Black's pieces.

19	...	♖c7
20	♗a6	

With the threat of 21 ♗b5.

20	...	♖c6

To answer 21 ♗b5 with

21...♖d6.

21	♕b3	♕b8

If 21...♖d6 22 ♖xd6 ♘xd6 23 c5 bxc5 24 ♖xc5 leaves Black badly tied up.

22	♕a4

With the idea of 23 ♖xd7.

22	...	♖c7
23	♕b5	♘f6
24	f3	d5
25	c5	h5

Andersson tries to deflect Karpov's attention from the queenside with ...h5-h4, but Karpov pursues his goal.

26	a4	♖e8
27	cxb6	axb6
28	a5	♖xc1
29	♖xc1	

Now if Black exchanges on a5, White exchanges queens and gains a winning advantage: 29...bxa5 30 ♕xb8 ♖xb8 31 bxa5 ♖a8 32 ♖c8+ ♖xc8 33 ♗xc8 ♘e8 34 a6 ♘c7 35 a7 ♔f8 36 ♗b7.

29	...	♕e5
30	♕xb6	d4
31	♔h1	♕e3
32	♖f1	e5
33	♗d3	

So that after 33...e4 34 dxe4 ♘xe4, 35 ♕b7 attacks f7.

33	...	h4
34	gxh4	♕f4
35	♖g1	

Avoiding the deadly threat 35 ...♘g4. Now 35...e4 is met by 36 ♕xd4.

35	...	♕xh4
36	a6	g6

36...e4 37 fxe4 ♘xe4 is met by 38 ♕c6 when Black has only a

few checks.

37   a7   ♔g7
38   ♗xg6   1-0

After 38 fxg6 39 a8(♕) ♖xa8 40 ♕b7+ wins and 38...♖h8 39 ♗e4+ ♔h6 40 a8(♕) wins.

Black should be able to obtain full equality if he keeps the centre closed and does not allow the white dark-squared bishop into play.

Now we move on to the fashionable 5 a3 variation, in which White forces Black to immediately relinquish one of his bishops.

Game 38
Figler-Dubinin
USSR 1975

---

1   d4   ♘f6
2   c4   e6
3   ♘f3   ♗b4+
4   ♘bd2   b6
5   a3   ♗xd2+
6   ♗xd2

Here 6 ♕xd2 is not dangerous after 6...♗b7 7 e3 (or 7 b4 a5) 7...0-0 8 b4 a5.

6   ...   ♗b7

6...h6 preventing the pin with 7 ♗g5, is considered later in the game Vaganian-Andersson.

7   g3

More critical is 7 ♗g5, which is considered in the next game. After the game continuation Black can play the conventional 7...0-0 or try a slightly unusual plan which leads to an interesting game.

7   ...   ♘c6

Black prevents 8 ♗g2 because of the threat of ...♘xd4 and 8 ♗g5 h6 9 ♗xf6 ♕xf6 still threatens ...♘xd4. Obviously White does not want to play e3 as this weakens the light squares, so he is forced to move his queen's bishop to an odd square.

8   ♗e3   d5

This is effective here as White cannot easily defend c4, and after 9 cxd5 ♘xd5 10 ♗g5 ♘de7 and White still has to worry about ...♘xd4.

9   ♗g2   dxc4
10   ♘e5   ♘d5
11   ♘xc4   ♕d7

Black prepares to castle queenside and then launch an

attack by ...h7-h5 and ...h5-h4.

| 12 | ♗c1 | 0-0-0 |
| 13 | e3 | h5 |

White does not want to castle on the kingside since ...h5-h4 would be dangerous.

14	b4	e5
15	dxe5	b5
16	♘a5	♘xa5
17	bxa5	♕f5

White is far behind in development and castling kingside is bad: 18 0-0 ♘c3 19 ♕b3 ♘e2+ 20 ♔h1 ♕f3 21 ♖g1 h4 22 gxh4

♖xh4 23 ♗xf3 ♗xf3+ 24 ♖g2 ♖xh2+ 25 ♔xh2 ♖h8+.

18	♕b3	♘c3
19	♗xb7+	♔xb7
20	a6+	♔c8
21	♕xc3	

Instead 21 0-0 ♘e2+ 22 ♔g2 h4 23 f3 hxg3 24 hxg3 ♕h3+ 25 ♔f2 ♕h2+ 26 ♔e1 ♕xg3+ 27 ♔xe2 ♖h2+ mates.

21	...	♕f3
22	♗b2	♕xh1+
23	♔e2	♕d5
24	♖c1	♖d7
25	♕b4	♖h6

0-1

White has no defence to ...♖c6 with the threat of ...♖xc1 followed by ...♕d1 mate. This game is well worth remembering.

Instead of 7 g3, White more often chooses 7 ♗g5, which can lead to very sharp play if Black decides to push back the bishop with ...h7-h6 and ...g7-g5.

Game 39
Nowak-Makarichev
Frunze 1986

1	d4	♘f6
2	c4	e6
3	♘f3	♗b4+
4	♘bd2	b6
5	a3	♗xd2+
6	♗xd2	♗b7
7	♗g5	d6
8	e3	♘bd7

A key juncture. In addition to the text move White can also try 9 ♗h4 (as in the next game, Karpov-Andersson), 9 ♗d3 (which leads to unclear play very similar to the text after 9...h6 10 ♗h4 g5 11 ♗g3 h5 12 h3 ♖g8) or even 9 ♕a4.

| 9 | ♗e2 | h6 |
| 10 | ♗h4 | |

10 ♗xf6 is clearly harmless.

10   ...   g5
11   ♗g3   h5

Black threatens ...h5-h4 winning a piece, so White is forced to play either 12 h3 or 12 h4.

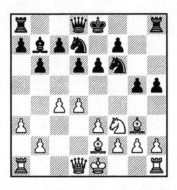

12   h4

White sacrifices a pawn. The alternative 12 h3 was seen in Shvidler-Ligterink, Amsterdam OHRA (B) 1988, but after 12...♖g8 13 ♖g1 h4 14 ♗h2 g4 15 ♘xh4 ♘e4 16 g3 gxh3 17 ♕c2 f5 Black held the advantage.

12   ...   g4
13   ♘g5   ♗xg2
14   ♖g1   ♗b7
15   f3

White aims to open up the f-file for an attack, but better is 15 ♕c2 preventing ...♘h7 when White has good compensation for the pawn.

15   ...   ♕e7

The alternatives were not promising: 15...gxf3 16 ♗xf3 ♗xf3 17 ♕xf3; or 15...♘h7 16 ♘xh7 ♖xh7 17 fxg4 both with good play for White.

16   ♖f1

After 16 fxg4 ♘xg4 17 ♗xg4 hxg4 18 ♕xg4 f5 19 ♕e2 ♘f6 Black has good control over e4.

16   ...   ♘h7

Not 16...0-0-0 17 fxg4 when Black cannot recapture on g4 with the knight because of ♖xf7.

17   ♘xh7   ♖xh7
18   ♕a4

Again after 18 fxg4 hxg4 19 ♗xg4 0-0-0 20 ♗f3 ♖g8 21 ♗xb7+ ♔xb7 22 ♕f3+ ♔b8 23 0-0-0 f5 Black has control of e4.

18   ...   0-0-0
19   ♕xa7   e5
20   c5

White has little choice: if 20 fxg4 exd4; 20 0-0-0 exd4; 20 fxg4 exd4; or 20 d5 gxf3 21 ♖xf3 ♖g7 22 ♗f2 ♘c5 23 0-0-0 ♔d7 threatening ...♖a8 trapping the queen.

20   ...   dxc5
21   d5

If 21 ♗a6 ♗xa6 22 ♕xa6+ ♔b8 23 a4 cxd4 24 a5 ♕b4+ followed by ...♘c5 wins for Black; and 21 dxe5 ♘xe5 22 ♗a6 ♗xa6 23 ♕xa6+ ♔b8 24 fxg4 ♖h6 leaves the white king dangerously exposed.

21   ...   c4
22   ♖c1

White must gain control of c4 for if 22 0-0-0 gxf3 23 ♖xf3 ♘f6 24 ♗xc4 ♕c5; or 22 ♗xc4 ♕c5.

22   ...   b5
23   fxg4

23 e4 gxf3 24 ♖xf3 gives White better chances than the game.

23	...	♘c5
24	♖f5	♖xd5
25	♗f3	e4

25...♘d3+ 26 ♔f1 e4 wins immediately.

26	♖xd5	♗xd5
27	♗e2	♖h6
28	b4	♘d3+
29	♗xd3	exd3
30	g5	♖b6

31	♔d2	♗b7
32	♖f1	c3+
33	♔xc3	♕xe3
34	♗f2	♖c6+
35	♔b3	♕e6+

0-1

The next game shows the long-term potential of the white bishop pair in the endgame.

Game 40
Karpov-Andersson
Skelleftea 1989

1	d4	♘f6
2	c4	e6
3	♘f3	♗b4+
4	♘bd2	b6
5	a3	♗xd2+
6	♗xd2	♗b7
7	♗g5	d6
8	e3	♘bd7
9	♗h4!?	

Prophylaxis; White retreats the bishop before he is forced to do so.

| 9 | ... | c5 |
| 10 | ♗d3 | |

10	...	0-0
11	0-0	cxd4
12	exd4	

On 12 ♘xd4 ♘e5 gives Black counterplay against the white c-pawn.

12	...	d5
13	♖e1	dxc4
14	♗xc4	♕c7

Also playable is 14...a6!? 15 a4 (15 ♖c1 b5 16 ♗a2 ♕b6 with counterplay) 15...♕c7.

| 15 | ♖c1 | ♖fc8! |

After 15...♖ac8 16 ♗g3 ♕d8 17 ♕d3 White has the initiative.

| 16 | ♖c3 | |

Not 16 ♖xe6 b5 17 ♖e8+ ♘xe8 18 ♗xf7+ ♔xf7 19 ♖xc7 ♖xc7 with advantage to Black.

16	...	♕d6
17	♗g3	♕f8
18	♕d3	a6

After 18...♘d5 19 ♘g5 ♘7f6 (19...g6 20 ♖c2) 20 ♗e5 ♘xc3 21 ♗xf6 ♘e4 22 ♖xe4 gxf6 23 ♖h4 ♕g7 White is in trouble

because of the potential threat against g2, but he can play 19 ♖c2 h6 20 ♘d2 ♘7f6 21 ♗e5 with the initiative.

19   ♘g5

White has unpleasant threats against f7 and e6 so Black exchanges and defends.

19	...	b5
20	♗a2	♖xc3
21	♕xc3	♗d5
22	♗b1	♖c8
23	♕e3	♕d8

This is rather too passive; a better try was 23...h6!? 24 ♘f3 (or 24 ♘h3 ♘b6 25 ♘f4 b4) 24...b4!? with counterplay for Black.

24	f3	♕b6
25	♕d2	a5
26	♗f2	b4
27	♖c1	♖xc1+
28	♕xc1	h6
29	♘h3!	

This is better than 29 ♘e4 bxa3 30 bxa3 ♗xe4 31 ♗xe4 (31 fxe4 ♘g4) 31...♘xe4 32 fxe4 ♕b7 with play against the white pawn on e4.

29	...	♕c6

Black should have played 29...bxa3 30 bxa3 ♕c6 31 ♕xc6 ♗xc6 with the idea of ...♘b6-c4 aiming at the pawn on a3.

30	♕xc6	♗xc6
31	axb4	axb4
32	♘f4	♘b6
33	b3	♘fd5
34	♘d3	♗b5
35	♗c2	♔f8
36	♗e1	♗xd3

If 36...♘c3 37 ♗xc3 bxc3 38 ♘b4 and White will round up the pawn on c3.

37	♗xd3	♔e7

White's two bishops offer him good winning prospects.

38	♔f2	♔d6
39	♗d2	♘d7
40	♗c4	

Not 40 ♔e2?! ♘b8! 41 ♗c4 ♘c6 42 ♔d3 ♘a5 attacking the pawn on b3.

40	...	♘7b6

Worthy of consideration is 40...♘b8!? 41 ♗xd5 ♔xd5 42 ♗xb4 g6 (42...♔xd4 43 ♗f8) 43 ♔e3 ♘c6 44 ♗c3 ♘a7 intending ...♘b5 and a blockade on the light squares.

41	♔e2	h5
42	♔d3	♔c6
43	g3	g6
44	♗xd5+	♘xd5
45	♔c4	f5
46	h3	♔b6
47	♗xb4	♘e3+
48	♔d3	♘d5
49	♗d2	♔b5
50	g4	♘f6 (D)

After 50...hxg4 51 fxg4 ♘f6 52 g5 ♘d5 53 h4 White should win because of the threat of obtaining a passed pawn with h5.

51	♗g5	♘d5
52	gxh5	gxh5
53	♗d2	♘f6
54	♔e3	♘d5+
55	♔f2	♘e7

Black must prevent the white king from entering on f4 or h4.

56	♗g5	♘c6

After 56...♘d5 57 ♔g3 ♔b4 58 ♔h4 ♔xb3 59 ♔xh5 ♔c4 60 ♔g6 ♔xd4 61 h4 wins.

57	♗f6	f4
58	♔e2	♔b4
59	♔d3	♔xb3
60	♔e4	♔c4
61	♗e5	♘e7
62	♗xf4	♘c6
63	♗e5	♘e7
64	h4	♘d5
65	♗h8!	♘e7
66	♗g7	♘g6

After 66...♘d5 67 ♔e5 wins.

67	♗f6	♘f8
68	♔e5	1-0

Black can also choose to prevent 7 ♗g5 by playing 6...h6, but this allows White time to gain control of e4 with ♗d3 and ♕c2.

Game 41
Vaganian-Andersson
Naestved 1985

1	d4	♘f6		2	c4	e6

3	♘f3	♗b4+
4	♘bd2	b6
5	a3	♗xd2+
6	♗xd2	h6
7	e3	♗b7
8	♗d3	d6

8...♘e4 is possible, with the idea of exchanging on d2 or supporting the knight with ...f7-f5.

| 9 | ♕c2 |

| 9 | ... | c5 |

Here Riemersma-Rogers, Wijk aan Zee (B) 1987, continued 9....♘bd7 10 b4 c5 11 dxc5 bxc5 12 ♗c3 0-0 13 0-0 ♕e7 14 ♘d2 ♖fc8 with a satisfactory game for Black.

10	dxc5!	bxc5
11	♗c3	♘bd7
12	0-0	a5
13	e4	0-0
14	♖ad1!

White now obtains a clear advantage; 14 e5?! ♘g4 15 exd6 ♗xf3 16 gxf3 ♕h4! gives Black attacking chances

| 14 | ... | ♕c7 |
| 15 | ♘h4 | ♕c6 |

After 15...♘e5 16 f4 ♘xd3 17 ♗xf6 ♗xe4 18 ♗c3 d5 19 ♖xd3 dxc4 20 ♖g3 ♗xc2 21 ♖xg7+ ♔h8 22 ♖xf7+ ♔g8 23 ♖xc7 White wins.

16	♖fe1	♘e5
17	♖e3	a4
18	♕d2	♖a7
19	f4?

19 ♖g3 ♔h8 20 ♖e1 with the threat of f4 would have been very hard for Black to meet.

19	...	♘xd3
20	♗xf6	♘xf4
21	♖g3?

Throwing away his attacking chances; after 21 ♕c3 d5 22 ♗xg7 d4 23 ♗xd4 cxd4 24 ♕xd4 ♖a5! leaves an unclear situation. In the rest of the game White goes steadily downhill in time-trouble.

21	...	♘g6
22	♖e1	♗c8
23	♖h3	e5
24	♘f5	♗xf5
25	exf5	♘f4
26	♖g3	g6
27	♖g4	♔h7
28	♖f1	♖g8
29	♕e3	♕d7
30	♖gxf4	exf4
31	♕xf4	gxf5
32	♗c3	0-1

As noted earlier 4 ♘bd2 is one of the most critical lines in the Bogo-Indian; 4...b6 should give Black enough counterplay for equality, but Black must play energetically and avoid endgames in which White has the two bishops.

3 4 ♘bd2; Systems with ...d7-d6 and ...e6-e5

In this chapter we look at the Black strategy of establishing a pawn chain in the centre with ...d7-d6 and ...e6-e5. It is likely that Black will have to exchange his king's bishop on d2 and thus leave White with the bishop pair; Black's intention is to block the dark-squared bishop out by placing his pawns on dark squares.

Game 42
Colle-Sämisch
Baden-Baden 1925

1	d4	♘f6
2	♘f3	e6
3	c4	♗b4+
4	♘bd2	0-0
5	a3	♗xd2+
6	♘xd2	

This move is well motivated, but perhaps too slow here as

Black has enough time to set up a solid defence against the white bishops. It is more accurate to recapture with 6 ♕xd2, which is considered in the next game, or 6 ♗xd2, when after 6...♘e4 7 g3 d6 8 ♗g2 ♘d7 9 0-0 f5 10 ♖c1 ♕e7 11 c5 White stood slightly better in Lputian-Psakhis, USSR Championship 1987.

6	...	d6
7	e3	e5
8	dxe5	dxe5
9	♕c2	♕e7
10	b3	

After 10 b4 a5 Black may gain control of the c5 square for his pieces, so White plays slowly.

10	...	c5
11	♗b2	♘c6
12	♗e2	

Instead 12 ♗d3 ♖e8 13 0-0 e4
14 ♗xf6 exd3 15 ♗xe7 dxc2 16
♗xc5 ♘e5 17 b4 ♘d3 18 ♘b3
♗e6 gives Black the advantage in
the endgame.

12	...	♗g4
13	♗f3	♖ac8
14	h3	♗xf3
15	gxf3	

After 15 ♘xf3 e4 16 ♘g5 h6
Black wins material so White
opts to recapture with the pawn to
play for an attack down the g-file.

15	...	♖fd8
16	♖g1	♖d6
17	♕f5	♖cd8
18	♕g5	g6
19	0-0-0	

19 ♘e4 ♘xe4 20 ♕xe7 ♘xe7
21 fxe4 ♘c6 leaves Black in
control of the d-file.

19	...	♖d3
20	♔c2	a6
21	♘b1	

Not 21 ♘e4 ♘xe4 22 ♕xe7
♖d2+ 23 ♖xd2 ♖xd2+ 24 ♔c1
♘xe7 25 fxe4 ♖xf2 with a winning endgame for Black.

21	...	♖xd1
22	♖xd1	♖xd1
23	♔xd1	♘d7
24	♕g2	♕e6
25	♘d2	f6 *(D)*

White's attack has disappeared
and now he must defend his weak
pawns in the endgame.

26	h4	♔f7
27	♕f1	♕f5
28	♔c1	h5
29	♕e2	♕h3
30	♕d3	♕e6
31	♘e4	♔e7

32	♗c3	a5
33	♗b2	b6
34	♘c3	♔f7
35	♘b5	♘e7
36	♔c2	♘f5
37	♕e4	♘d6
38	♘xd6+	♕xd6

The exchange of knights leaves
the white kingside pawns to be
picked off.

39	♕a8	♕e7
40	♕e4	♕e6
41	♕d3	♘f8
42	e4	♕d7
43	♕e3	♕h3
44	♕d2	♕xf3
45	♕d5+	♔e7
46	♗c1	♕xf2+
47	♔b1	♕xh4
48	♗h6	♘d7
49	♕g8	♕xe4+

Black has devoured the white
kingside and now moves on to the
queenside pawns.

50	♔a2	♕c2+
51	♔a1	♕xb3
52	♕g7+	♔d6
53	♕f7	♕xa3+
54	♔b1	♕d3+

55	♔a1	h4
56	♗f8+	♔c7
57	♕h7	h3
	0-1	

White can also recapture on move six with the queen which, as we shall see, presents Black with more problems.

Game 43
Browne-Agdestein
Gjovik 1983

1	d4	♘f6
2	c4	e6
3	♘f3	♗b4+
4	♘bd2	0-0
5	a3	♗xd2+
6	♕xd2	♕e7
7	e3	d6

Black prepares his central thrust ...e6-e5, which will enable him to develop his queen's bishop.

| 8 | b4 |

White takes the opportunity to gain space on the queenside while preparing to develop his queen's bishop on b2.

8	...	e5
9	dxe5!	dxe5
10	♗b2	

White pressurizes the black pawn on e5, which is awkward for Black. If Black advances with ...e5-e4 then White obtains a terrific diagonal for his queen's bishop.

| 10 | ... | ♘bd7 |
| 11 | ♕c3 | ♖e8 |

Although 11 ... ♘e4 12 ♕c2 ♘ef6 is also possible, Black's best alternative seems 11...e4 12 ♘e5 a5 13 ♘xd7 ♗xd7 14 ♗e2 axb4 15 axb4 ♖xa1+ 16 ♗xa1 c5 17 b5 ♖a8 as in Browne-Larsen, Mar del Plata 1981.

12	c5	e4
13	♘d2	♘e5
14	♘c4	♘g6

Here White has the advantage

because of his pressure down the long diagonal.

15	♗e2	♗e6
16	♖d1	♖ad8
17	0-0	♖d5
18	♖xd5	♗xd5
19	♖d1	♕e6

So White cannot use the open d-file, but now Browne turns his attention to the queenside where he can break through with a pawn advance.

| 20 | b5 | ♕f5 |

Black is hoping to gain a king-side attack with ...♕g5 and ...♘h4, but White strikes first.

| 21 | b6 | ♗xc4 |
| 22 | ♕xc4 | |

Now if Black plays 22...axb6 23 cxb6 cxb6 24 ♕d4 is good for

White, since Black is badly tied down to the defence of g7.

22	...	♘g4?
23	♗xg4	♕xg4
24	♕a4	c6
25	h3	

White must drive the black queen away. If instead 25 bxa7 ♘h4 26 g3 ♘f3+ Black generates some counterplay.

25	...	♕h5
26	bxa7	♘f8
27	♖b1	♖a8
28	♗d4	♕f5
29	♖xb7	♕c8
30	♕b3	♘d7
31	a4	1-0

The next game also shows the advantage of the two bishops.

Game 44
Miles-Short
Manchester 1982

1	d4	♘f6		4	♘bd2	0-0
2	c4	e6		5	e3	d6
3	♘f3	♗b4+		6	♗e2	

6 a3 ♗xd2+ 7 ♗xd2 ♕e7 was considered in the game P. Littlewood-Short in the Positional Themes chapter.

6	**...**	**♘bd7**
7	**0-0**	

White has developed simply and now threatens to play 8 ♘b3 followed by a2-a3 trapping the bishop, so Short decides to exchange.

7	**...**	**♗xd2**
8	**♘xd2**	

An interesting recapture. Black is planning to advance in the centre with ...e6-e5 and possibly ...e5-e4, so Miles takes the sting out of this advance.

8	**...**	**e5**
9	**b3 (D)**	
9	**...**	**exd4**
10	**exd4**	**d5**
11	**♗f3**	**♖e8**

Black is hoping to create a strong point on d5 for his pieces, but Miles stops this plan.

12	**cxd5**	**♘b6**
13	**d6!**	

A fine move that prevents Black from recapturing on d5 with a knight, after which his position would be secure.

13	**...**	**♕xd6**
14	**♘c4**	

Now if Black exchanges on c4 then after 14...♘xc4 15 bxc4 White has the bishop pair and the semi-open b-file to use.

14	**...**	**♕e6**
15	**♘xb6**	**axb6**
16	**d5**	**♕e5**
17	**♗e3**	

Black has some difficulties because of the weakness of his pawn on c7, but he could put up stiffer resistance with 17...♗f5 keeping his pieces active.

17	**...**	**♖d8**
18	**♗d4**	**♕d6**
19	**♗xf6**	

Surprisingly giving up the strong dark-squared bishop, but it enables White to force a weakness. If Black recaptures with the queen then White builds up on the c-pawn after 19...♕xf6 20 ♕c2 ♕d6 21 ♖ac1.

19	**...**	**gxf6**

20	♕c2	♗d7
21	♖fd1	♖e8
22	♖ac1	♖ac8
23	♗e4	

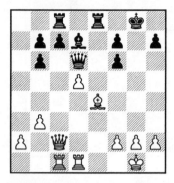

Having tied down pieces to the defence Miles turns his attention to Black's weakened king's position.

23	...	♔g7
24	♗f5	♖cd8
25	g3	♗xf5
26	♕xf5	♖e5
27	♕g4+	♖g5
28	♕f3	

Now if Black takes the d-pawn he loses in the rook ending:

28...♖xd5 29 ♖xd5 ♕xd5 30 ♕xd5 ♖xd5 31 ♖xc7 ♖d2 32 ♖xb7 ♖xa2 33 ♖xb6 when White has a strong passed pawn and Black's kingside pawns are very weak.

28	...	♖e8
29	♖c4	

29 h4 is best, not allowing Black to double his rooks on the fourth rank.

29	...	♖ee5!
30	h4	♖ef5!

Not 30...♖exd5 31 ♖dc1 ♖gf5 32 ♕g4+ ♔h6 33 ♖xc7 with advantage to White.

31	♕e2	

Not 31 ♕e3 ♖xd5 32 ♖dc1 ♖ge5!.

31	...	♖xd5
32	♖dc1	♖d2
33	♕f3	♖d3
34	♕xd3	♕xd3
35	hxg5	fxg5
36	♖xc7	

White has the advantage with his two rooks against the black queen. He can attack the pawns on the queenside twice with his rooks, whereas Black can only defend them once with his queen. Black must try to obtain counterplay by opening up the white king with the advance of his kingside pawns.

36	...	♛d2
37	♖1c2	♛d1+
38	♔h2	h5

38...b5 was a good alternative, preventing White from obtaining a post on c4 for his rook.

39	a4	♔g6
40	♖7c4	h4
41	gxh4	gxh4
42	♖2c3	♔g5
43	♖h3	

43	...	♛d6+
44	♔g1	♛d1+
45	♔g2	♛d5+
46	♖f3	

This looks very risky, but it enables White to round up the h-pawn.

46	...	h3+
47	♔g3	f5
48	♖cc3	♛d1
49	♔h2	f4

Or 49...♛f1 50 ♖g3+ ♔f4 51 ♖c2 with the threat of taking on h3.

50	♖xh3	♛f1
51	♖hf3	♔g4
52	♖cd3	b5

The alternative 52...♛e2 53 ♔g2 ♛e4 54 ♔f1 ♛xf3 55 ♖xf3 ♔xf3 56 ♔e1 ♔e4 57 ♔e2 ♔d4 58 ♔f3 ♔c3 59 ♔xf4 ♔xb3 60 ♔e5 ♔xa4 61 f4 b5 62 f5 b4 63 ♔d4 b3 64 ♔c3 ♔a3 65 f6 b2 66 f7 b1(♛) 67 f8(♛)+ ♔a4 68 ♛a8+ ♔b5 69 ♛xb7+ wins for White.

53	axb5	b6
54	♖c3	♛xb5
55	♖fd3	♛e5
56	f3+	♔h4
57	♖c2	♛f5
58	♖cd2	♛h3+
59	♔g1	♔g3
60	♖f2	b5
61	♖d8	♛h7
62	♖g8+	1-0

After 62...♛xg8 63 ♖g2+ wins the queen.

The evidence of this chapter suggests that the strategy of ...d7-d6 and ...e6-e5 is insufficient for Black to obtain an equal game since it is hard to stifle White's powerful dark-squared bishop.

4 4 ♘bd2; Other Systems

In the previous two chapters we have looked at two systems whereby Black delays striking directly in the centre after 4 ♘bd2. Here we shall look at the two ways in which Black can claim an immediate stake in the centre. After 4...d5 Black can later retreat the bishop to e7 if he wishes, whereas after 4...c5 he is almost committed to exchanging the king's bishop. First we shall discuss the latter possibility.

The sharp 4...c5 has been championed by the Dutch grandmaster Jan Timman, among others.

1	d4	♘f6
2	c4	e6
3	♘f3	♗b4+
4	♘bd2	c5
5	e3	0-0
6	a3	♗xd2+
7	♕xd2	*(D)*

You will recall that we have already seen an example of this line in the Positional Themes chapter (Dahlberg-Korchnoi), where we saw Black continue with the plan of fianchettoing his queen's bishop. Timman opts for a completely different scheme of development.

7	...	cxd4
8	♘xd4	

The natural 8 exd4 is considered in the next game.

| 8 | ... | ♘c6 |

Again 8...d5 is worth consideration: 9 cxd5 ♕xd5 10 ♘f3 b6

with good play.

| 9 | ♗e2 | e5 |

9...d5 10 ♘xc6 bxc6 11 cxd5 cxd5 12 b4 concedes White the advantage due to his two bishops.

| 10 | ♘xc6 |

10 ♘b5 d5 11 cxd5 ♘xd5 leads to an equal position.

| 10 | ... | dxc6 |
| 11 | f3 |

A good move, preventing the black knight jumping into e4. Instead 11 0-0 ♕xd2 12 ♗xd2 ♘e4 is equal.

| 11 | ... | ♕e7 |
| 12 | b3 | e4 |

Black starts active play while White is still completing his development.

| 13 | ♗b2 | ♖d8 |
| 14 | ♕b4 |

The exchange of queens would favour White with his two bishops, so Timman avoids the swap.

14	...	c5
15	♕c3	exf3
16	gxf3

Or 16 ♗xf3 ♗f5 17 ♗d5 ♗e4 18 ♖d1 ♗xd5 19 cxd5 ♖e8 with good play for Black.

16	...	♘h5
17	h4	♗f5
18	♔f2

Now White has the two bishops and the open g-file, but his king is slightly unsafe.

18	...	♖d6
19	♕e5	♕xe5
20	♗xe5	♖e6
21	♗h2!

White now threatens 22 e4 followed by 23 ♗d3 with the advantage, so Timman retreats his bishop.

| 21 | ... | ♗g6 |

Now 22 e4 can be answered by 22...f5.

| 22 | ♖hc1 |

Best is 22 ♖he1 ♖ae8 23 ♗f1 with the idea of ♗h3 retaining the advantage for White.

| 22 | ... | ♖ae8 |
| 23 | ♖c3 | ♖a6! |

This move prevents White from advancing on the queenside with b4.

24	♖cc1	♖ae6
25	♖c3	♖a6
26	a4	♖d8
27	♖d1	♖xd1
28	♗xd1	♘f6

This move is very useful. White was threatening 29 e4 followed by occupying the d-file by ♖d3, but now this is impossible because of the tactical trick 29...♗xe4 30 fxe4 ♘xe4+.

29	♔e1	♘d7
30	e4	♔f8
31	♖d3	♔e7
32	♖d5	f6
33	♔d2	

This blocks the activity of the white rook; more to the point was 33 ♗c2.

33	...	♗f7
34	♖d3	♘e5

Black has skilfully extracted himself from a slightly worse ending. White cannot exchange bishop for knight as his kingside pawns would then be disastrously weak.

35	♖e3	♖d6+
36	♔c2	♖d8
37	♗e2	♘c6
38	♔c3	

Black could now take the initiative with 38...♘d4 39 ♗d1 ♗h5 when White is tied down to the f-pawn.

38	...	♘b4
39	f4	♔f8
40	f5	

40 h5 was better.

40	...	♘c6
41	♗f3	½-½

After 41...♘e5 42 ♗xe5 fxe5 43 ♖d3 ♖xd3+ 44 ♔xd3 ♔e7 the endgame is slightly better for Black but not winning; 43...♖d4 44 ♖xd4 cxd4 45 ♔b4 ♔e7 46 ♔c5 ♔d7 47 a5 is good for a draw for White .

Timman has continued to play 4...c5 with success, and has even used it against the world champion.

Game 46
Kasparov-Timman
Brussels 1987

1	d4	♘f6		3	♘f3	♗b4+
2	c4	e6		4	♘bd2	c5

5   e3

5	...	0-0
6	a3	♗xd2+
7	♕xd2	cxd4
8	exd4	b6
9	♗e2?!	

9 b4!, expanding on the queenside, was more accurate, and if 9...d5 10 c5 with a space advantage.

| 9 | ... | d5! |

Now if 10 c5 bxc5 11 dxc5 a5 with good play for Black.

10	b3	♗a6
11	♕b2!	dxc4
12	bxc4	♘c6

Also playable is 12...♕c7 13 ♘e5 ♘bd7 14 ♗f4 with equality.

| 13 | ♗g5 | ♖c8! |

After 13...h6 14 ♗h4 g5?! 15

♗g3 g4?! White can sacrifice a piece with 16 ♗h4! gxf3 17 gxf3 when he has good compensation according to Kasparov. After the text move Black even stands slightly better.

| 14 | ♖d1 | |

After 14 ♖c1 h6 15 ♗h4 g5 16 ♗g3 ♘e4 Black has good play.

14	...	♘a5
15	c5	♗xe2
16	♕xe2	♕d5

Here also 16...h6 17 ♗h4 ♕d5 18 ♗xf6 gxf6 19 cxb6 axb6 20 0-0 ♔h7 is fine for Black.

17	♗xf6	gxf6
18	cxb6	axb6
19	0-0	♖c3
20	♕d2	♖xa3
21	♕f4	♔g7
22	♕g4+	

Instead 22 ♘e5 h6! 23 ♘g4 ♕g5 gives Black good chances.

| 22 | ... | ♔h8 |
| 23 | ♕f4 | |

Not 23 ♕h4?? ♖xf3 winning.

23	...	♔g7
24	♕g4+	♔h8
25	♕f4	½-½

If White captures on c5 then Black can also gain counterplay by the threat of ...♘e4.

Game 47
Hertneck-Christiansen
Munich 1991

1	d4	♘f6
2	c4	e6
3	♘f3	♗b4+

| 4 | ♘bd2 | c5 |
| 5 | a3 | |

Immediately forcing the

exchange of Black's bishop.

5   ...   ♗xd2+
6   ♕xd2

The other sensible recapture is 6 ♗xd2, when after 6...cxd4 7 ♘xd4 Black tried to simplify with 7...d5 in Lobron-Korchnoi, Biel 1986, but ran into 8 cxd5 ♕xd5 9 e3 0-0 10 ♗b4 ♖d8 11 ♗e7 ♖d7 12 ♗xf6 gxf6 13 ♕g4+ ♔f8 and Black's shattered kingside promised White the better game.

6   ...   0-0

An interesting pawn sacrifice; previously 6...b6 (transposing to Kasparov-Timman after 7 e3) and 6...cxd4 (which is best met by 7 b4! 0-0 8 ♗b2) were the standard choices.

7   dxc5

White takes up the challenge instead of setting for 7 e3 transposing to the previous games.

7   ...   a5

Clearly Black must prevent White from playing b4; the immediate 7...♘e4 8 ♕c2 ♘xc5 9 b4 is unattractive.

8   g3   a4

Fixing White's queenside once and for all.

9	♕c2	♘c6
10	♗g2	♕a5+
11	♗d2	♕xc5

Black has regained the pawn with at least equality due to the hole on b3.

12	♖c1	b5
13	cxb5	♕xb5
14	0-0	♗b7
15	e4	♖ac8
16	♗c3	♘e7
17	♘d4	♕a6
18	♖fe1	e5
19	♘f3	d6
20	♘d2	♖fe8
21	♗f1	♕a8
22	♗b5	♗c6
23	♕d3	♘g6
24	♗xc6	♖xc6
25	♖cd1	♕c8
26	♘f1	h5
27	♘e3	♖d8
28	h4	♖d7
29	♖d2	♘e7
30	♖ed1	♖b7
31	♔g2	♖b3
32	f3	♘d7
33	♕e2	♕c7
34	♗b4 *(D)*	

White aims to capture the pawn on d6 but Black is ready with an exchange sacrifice

34	...	♘c5
35	♘c4	♖xb4
36	axb4	♘xe4
37	♘a5	♘xd2
38	♘xc6	♘xc6
39	♕xd2	♘d4

Black has good compensation

for the sacrificed exchange in view of White's weak pawns.

40	♕c3	♕b7
41	♔f2	g6
42	♖xd4	exd4
43	♕xd4	♕c6
44	♔e3	♕c1+
45	♕d2	♕g1+
46	♔f4	♕b1
47	♔e3	♕g1+

48	♔f4	♕b6
49	♕c3	d5
50	g4	hxg4
51	♔xg4	d4
52	♕c5	♕xc5
53	bxc5	f5+
	0-1	

Now we turn to the system with 4...d5 (or 4...0-0 and a later ...d7-d5) in which Black retains the option of retreating his bishop to e7, reaching a position similar to the Queen's Gambit but with the white knight on d2 rather than c3. This should be advantageous to Black because there is not so much pressure on his centre, but since Black has wasted some time on moving his king's bishop, White may be able to use this to gain an initiative on the queenside with b4.

Game 38
Li Zunian-Hernandez
Lucerne (Olympiad) 1982

1	d4	♘f6
2	c4	e6
3	♘f3	♗b4+
4	♘bd2	d5 *(D)*

As noted above, Black often plays 4...0-0, which will transpose to the variations considered below if Black follows up with ...d7-d5.

5 e3

The naive-looking 5 ♕a4+ ♘c6 6 ♘e5 ♗d7 7 ♘xc6 ♗xd2+ 8 ♗xd2 ♗xc6 9 ♕c2 0-0 leads to

a satisfactory position for Black, and also perfectly satisfactory for Black is 5 a3 ♗e7 6 ♕c2 b6 7 e4 dxe4 8 ♘xe4 ♗b7 9 ♗d3 ♘c6! 10 ♗e3 ♘g4 11 0-0 f5, as in Yusupov-Spassky, Barcelona 1989.

5   ...   0-0
6   ♗d3

Often 6 a3 is played here, though this allows Black the possibility of 6...♗e7 7 ♗d3 c5, with equal chances.

6   ...   b6

Also perfectly playable is 6...dxc4 7 ♗xc4 ♘c6 with the idea of retreating the bishop to d6 (after a2-a3) and playing ...e6-e5.

7   a3   ♗e7

Here 7...♗xd2+ 8 ♗xd2 ♗a6 would transpose to the game Pytel-Plachetka, which was discussed in the chapter on positional themes.

8   0-0   ♗b7
9   cxd5

An interesting strategic decision. White could also try 9 b3, which is covered in the next game, or 9 b4 c5 10 bxc5 bxc5 11 ♖b1 ♕c8 12 ♕b3 ♗a6 13 ♗b2 ♘bd7 14 ♖fc1 ♖b8, which led to an equal position in Miles-Korchnoi, Lucerne (Olympiad) 1982, but the immediate exchange on d5 presents Black with a more difficult task. If Black recaptures on d5 with a piece then e3-e4 will win a tempo; and if Black recaptures with the pawn then after 10 b4 a subsequent ... c7-c5, bxc5 bxc5, dxc5 will leave Black with an isolated d-pawn.

9   ...   exd5
10   b4   c6

Now Black threatens 11...a5 12 b5 c5 with good play.

11   ♘b3!   ♘bd7

If 11...a5 12 bxa5 bxa5 13 ♗d2 and White has a good game.

12   ♗b2   ♖e8
13   ♖c1

White has a positional advantage because of his pressure down the half-open c-file.

13   ...   ♗d6
14   ♕e2

White intends to exchange the light-squared bishops to weaken the black c-pawn.

14   ...   a6
15   ♘h4

Threatening to invade on f5. Black is obviously loathe to weaken his king's position with ...g7-g6, but this would have been better than allowing the knight to f5.

15   ...   ♘e4?
16   ♘f5   ♗f8
17   f3   ♘d6
18   ♘xd6   ♗xd6

19   e4

White threatens to continue with e5 and f4, creating a powerful pawn roller on the kingside.

19	...	♗f4
20	♖c2	♕g5
21	♗c1	f5
22	♗xf4	♕xf4
23	e5	

Now White cannot be prevented from cementing his centre with g3 and f4.

23	...	g6
24	a4	h5
25	g3	♕h6
26	f4	

White has a big advantage due to his vastly superior bishop and Black's weak queenside.

26	...	♘f8
27	a5	b5
28	♘c5	♗c8
29	♕f3	♖a7

29...♘e6 is not possible due to 30 ♘xe6 ♖xe6 31 ♖xc6 ♖xc6 32 ♕xd5+.

30	h3	♖g7
31	♖g2	

White is intending a breakthrough with g4.

31	...	♖ee7
32	♗e2	♖ef7
33	♕e3	♘e6
34	♘xe6	♗xe6
35	♕c3	♗d7

Now White decides to give up his strong passed e-pawn in order to win the black queenside.

36	e6	♗xe6
37	♕xc6	

Black must either lose material with no hope of saving the game or try for active play.

37	...	g5
38	♗f3	♕f6

39	fxg5	Rxg5
40	h4	Rgg7
41	Bxh5	Wxd4+
42	Kh2	Rf6
43	Rf4	

Black has maintained material equality but his army is badly disjointed.

43	...	We3
44	Wxa6	Kh7
45	Wd6	Rh6
46	Bf3	Rhg6
47	Wb6	We1

If Black exchanges queens with 47...Wxb6 48 axb6 Rb7 49 Rd4 Rxb6 50 Bxd5 Rd6 51 Rgd2 Bxd5 52 Rxd5Rxd5 53 Rxd5 his pawns disappear.

48	Wg1	We5
49	Wd4	We1
50	Rg1	1-0

The queen has no escape.

If White retains the tension then Black should be able to equalize easily enough.

Game 49
Bisguier-Matanovic
Bled 1961

1	d4	Nf6
2	c4	e6
3	Nf3	Bb4+
4	Nbd2	d5
5	a3	Be7
6	e3	0-0
7	Bd3	b6
8	0-0	Bb7
9	b3	

As we saw in the previous game, 9 cxd5 gives Black more problems.

9	...	c5 *(D)*
10	Bb2	Nbd7
11	We2	dxc4

Black resolves the tension in the centre.

12	Nxc4	cxd4
13	Nxd4	Nc5
14	Bc2	Wd5
15	f3	Ba6
16	Rad1	Bxc4
17	bxc4	Wb7

18	Nb5	a6
19	Nc3	Rfd8
20	e4	Rxd1
21	Rxd1	Rd8
22	e5	Rxd1+
23	Wxd1	Nfd7
24	f4	g6
25	We2	f5
26	exf6	Bxf6

Black's position is preferable

due to his solid knight on c5.

27	♘d1	♕c7
28	♗xf6	♘xf6
29	♕d2	♕d7
30	♕xd7	♘fxd7
31	♔f2	♔f7
32	♔e3	♔e7
33	g4	e5
34	h4	exf4+
35	♔xf4	♘e6+
36	♔g3	♔f6
37	♗e4	♔e5
38	♗d5	♘f4
39	♗f3	h6
40	♘e3	♘c5
41	h5	gxh5
42	gxh5	♘e4+
43	♔h4	♘f6
44	♗b7	a5
45	♗f3	♘e6
46	♗g4	♘d4
47	c5	b5 *(D)*

The black pawns are more dangerous than the white c-pawn as they are further from the respective kings.

48	♗d1	♔e4
49	♘g4	♘g8
50	♔g3	♔d5

51	♔f4	♔xc5

Black has won material but victory is still far from being a formality.

52	♔e3	♔c4
53	♔d2	b4
54	axb4	♔xb4
55	♔d3	♘b3
56	♔c2	a4
57	♔b2	a3+
58	♔a2	♘d4
59	♘e5	♘b5
60	♘c6+	♔c5
61	♘e5	♘f6
62	♗e2	♘c3+
63	♔xa3	♘xe2
64	♘f7	♘g4
65	♔b3	♔d4
66	♔b4	♘c3
67	♔b3	♘d5
68	♘xh6	♘xh6

Black has just enough time to win this endgame.

69	♔a2	♔e3
70	♔b3	♔d3
71	♔b2	♘b4
72	♔b3	♘c2
73	♔a4	♔c4
74	♔a5	♔c5

75	♔a4	♘d4
76	♔a3	♔b5
77	♔b2	♔b4
78	♔a2	♘c2
79	♔b2	♘e3

80	♔a2	♘c4
81	♔b1	♔c3
82	♔a2	♔c2
83	♔a1	♘a3
84	♔a2	♘b1
85	♔a1	♘f5
86	♔a2	♘d4
87	h6	♘b3
88	h7	♘c1+
89	♔a1	♘d2
	0-1	

90 h8(♕) ♘db3 is mate.

As we have said Black can also play the provocative 4...0-0, tempting White to expand in the centre with 5 a3 ♗e7 6 e4 d5 with very sharp play.

Game 50
Browne-Makarichev
Saint John 1988

1	d4	♘f6
2	c4	e6
3	♘f3	♗b4+
4	♘bd2	0-0
5	a3	♗e7
6	e4	

6 e3 d5 leads to positions discussed earlier in this chapter.

| 6 | ... | d5 *(D)* |
| 7 | ♗d3 | |

7 e5 ♘fd7 8 cxd5 exd5 9 ♗d3 (9 b4 a5 10 b5 is interesting) 9...c5 amounts to nothing more than a transposition, but A. Petrosian-Ulibin, Pavlodar 1987, went instead 7 cxd5 exd5 8 e5 ♘e4!? (8...♘fd7 9 ♗d3 c5 again transposes to the text game) 9 ♗d3 f5

10 0-0 c5 11 dxc5 a5 12 ♘b3?! (12 ♕c2 would have been an improvement) 12...♘c6 13 ♗b5 f4 when Black developed a strong kingside attack as follows: 14

♘bd4 ♘xd4 15 ♘xd4 ♗xc5 16
♘b3 ♗b6 17 ♗e2 ♘g3 18 ♖e1
♕h4 19 ♗f3 ♘e4 20 ♕xd5+ ♔h8
21 ♕xe4 ♗xf2+ 22 ♔f1 ♗f5 23
♕e2 ♗b6 24 ♖d1 ♖ad8 25 ♖xd8
♖xd8 26 g3 fxg3 27 hxg3 ♕xg3
28 ♗e3 ♗d3 0-1.

Another interesting idea for
White in this variation is 7 ♕c2,
intending to meet 7...c5 with 8
dxc5 a5 9 cxd5 exd5 10 ♗d3,
maintaining the tension in the
centre. Black might try 7...dxe4
8 ♘xe4 ♘c6 9 ♗d3 h6, when 10
♗e3 can be met by 10...♘g4.

7	...	c5
8	cxd5	exd5
9	e5	♘fd7
10	0-0	♘c6
11	♖e1	a5
12	♕c2	

Neither is 12 ♗c2 dangerous
for Black after 12...♖e8 13 ♘f1
cxd4 14 ♘g3 ♘f8 15 ♘xd4 ♗c5,
as in Hertneck-Hecht, Munich
1988.

12	...	h6
13	♘f1	

More accurate is 13 ♗f5 cxd4
14 ♘b3, as in Piket-
Brenninkmeijer, Groningen 1988,
when after 14...♕b6 15 e6 White
stood slightly better.

13	...	cxd4
14	♘g3	♘c5
15	♗f5	a4
16	♗f4	d3
17	♗xd3	♗g4
18	♖ad1	♘e6

White is in great difficulties
because of the threat of ...♘d4.

19	♕d2	♗xf3

20	gxf3	♘cd4
21	♕e3	g5

Trapping the white bishop on
f4. White attempts to checkmate
Black on h7 but he does not have
enough time.

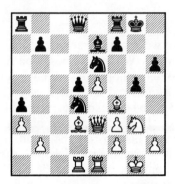

22	♗b1	gxf4
23	♕d3	♘g5

White must waste a move preventing the knight fork on f3.

24	♔h1	fxg3
25	f4	g2+
26	♔xg2	♘de6
27	♕g3	♔h8
28	fxg5	♗xg5
29	♔h1	♖g8
30	♕f3	♗f4
31	♕d3	♖g7
32	♕h3	♕g5
33	♖g1	♕xe5
34	♖xg7	♕xg7
35	♖g1	♕e5
	0-1	

In conclusion, although the
systems with ...c7-c5 and ...d7-d5
offer Black chances of equality,
4...b6 is probably the most reliable reply to 4 ♘bd2.

5 4 ♗d2 a5; Black plays ...b7-b6

Here we begin our survey of lines in which White interposes on d2 with his bishop. First we consider the sequence 1 d4 ♘f6 2 c4 e6 3 ♘f3 ♗b4+ 4 ♗d2 a5. With this move Black supports his advanced bishop on b4, and if White exchanges bishops, the development of the knight on c3 is prevented by the black pawn on b4 and Black has good play down the half-open a-file. If Black later decides to exchange the bishop on b4 then ...a7-a5 is still a useful move, holding up White's queenside pawn advance with b2-b4.

In this chapter we shall look at games where Black fianchettoes his queen's bishop. This can be met by White in one of two ways: either by developing the bishop on d3 after playing e2-e3 or by a kingside fianchetto. Let us first discuss the system of classical development with e2-e3 and ♗d3.

Game 41
Kasparov-Tal
Niksic 1983

1	d4	♘f6
2	c4	e6
3	♘f3	♗b4+
4	♗d2	a5
5	♘c3	b6
6	e3	♗b7
7	♗d3 *(D)*	

White has developed simply and is now planning ♕c2 followed by pushing in the centre with e2-e4. How should Black react to this? If 7...♗xc3 8 ♗xc3 ♘e4 9 ♗xe4 ♗xe4 10 d5 and White has the advantage because of his strong bishop on c3. Tal decides instead that he cannot prevent e4 so must blockade on e5.

7	...	d6
8	♕c2	♘bd7
9	e4	e5
10	♘d5!	

Instead 10 0-0 0-0 11 ♖fe1 exd4 12 ♘xd4 ♗c5 gives Black a satisfactory game

10	...	♗xd2+
11	♕xd2	exd4

Black need not surrender the centre; 11...c6 12 ♘c3 leaves White with a slight advantage.

12	♘xd4	♘c5
13	0-0	0-0
14	♖fe1!	

If White had defended e4 by 14 f3 then Black has a tactical possibility at his disposal: 14...c6 15 ♘c3 ♘xd3 16 ♕xd3 d5 17 cxd5 ♗a6 18 ♕d2 cxd5 19 e5 ♗xf1 20 exf6 ♗a6 with an unclear position.

14	...	♖e8

Here 14 ... c6 seems more prudent as now White could have played 15 ♘f5 with two possible continuations: 15...♘fxe4 16 ♗xe4 ♘xe4 (16...♖xe4!?) 17 ♕d4 ♕g5 18 ♖xe4 ♕xf5 19 ♖g4 ♕e5 20 ♘f6+ ♔h8 21 ♘xe8 ♖xe8 with advantage to White; or 15...♗xd5 16 cxd5 ♘xd3 17 ♕xd3 again with advantage to White.

15	f3	c6
16	♘c3	♕c7

Black cannot break out with 16...d5 17 cxd5 cxd5 18 e5 ♘fd7 19 f4 ♘xd3 20 ♕xd3 ♘c5 21 ♕g3 when White is threatening on the kingside.

17	♗f1	♖ad8

18	♖ad1?	

Better would have been 18 ♘f5 threatening 19 ♘xg7 and ♕xg5+; after 18...♘e6 19 ♖ad1 d5 20 cxd5 cxd5 21 e5 White has a clear advantage because of the weak black d-pawn.

18	...	d5
19	cxd5	cxd5
20	♘cb5	♕b8
21	e5	

Or 21 ♘f5 dxe4 22 ♘bd6 4e6 23 ♕f2 exf3 24 ♘xe8 ♖xe8 when Black has compensation for the exchange.

21	...	♖xe5
22	♖xe5	♕xe5
23	♖e1	♕b8
24	♘f5	

Now White threatens ♕g5 winning.

24	...	♘e6
25	♘bd4	♖e8

Worth considering is 25...♕f4 26 ♖e3!? with an unclear position.

26	♗b5	♘xd4
27	♖xe8+	♘xe8
28	♕xd4	♕c7!
29	♗xe8	♕c1+
30	♔f2	♕c2+
31	♔e3	♕xf5
32	♕xb6	♕g5+
33	♔d3	½-½

After 33...♕xg2 34 ♗xf7+ ♔xf7 35 ♕xb7+ ♔e6 neither side has any advantage. An excellent fighting game.

If White plays more slowly then Black can establish a firm footing in the centre.

Game 42
Malich-Smyslov
Berlin 1979

1	d4	♘f6
2	c4	e6
3	♘f3	♗b4+
4	♗d2	a5
5	♘c3	b6
6	e3	♗b7
7	♗d3	d6

So far all is as in Kasparov-Tal, but now White tries a different, slower strategy.

8	a3?!	♗xc3
9	♗xc3	♘e4

Now 10 ♗xe4 ♗xe4 11 d5 e5 is perfectly satisfactory, since the c3 bishop is blocked.

10	♖c1	♕e7
11	0-0	♘xc3
12	♖xc3	e5

Black threatens ...e5-e4 winning a piece, so White must retreat.

13	♗c2	e4

Black closes the centre in order to attack the white king.

14	♘d2	0-0
15	b4	♘d7
16	♕b1	♘f6
17	♖c1	♖fe8

Smyslov overprotects his e-pawn and prepares a kingside attack with ...h5-h4-h3.

18	♗b3	

Instead 18 ♗d1 axb4 19 axb4 c5 20 ♗e2 ♖a7 leaves Black with a slight advantage.

18	...	axb4
19	axb4	c5
20	♗d1	cxd4
21	exd4	b5!

Black sacrifices a pawn in order to obtain the d5 square for his knight, after which he will be able to attack with ...e4-e3.

22	c5	♘d5
23	♖g3	e3
24	fxe3	♘xe3
25	♗f3	♗xf3
26	♘xf3	♘d5

Black retreats his knight in order to defend against White's threats, but this is only a temporary backward step.

27	♘g5	♘f6
28	♖b3	

The desperate 28 ♖f1 h6 29 ♖xf6 ♕xf6 30 ♕h7+ ♔f8 leads to nothing for White.

| 28 | ... | ♕e2 |

With the deadly threat of ... ♖a2.

29	♖c2	♕g4
30	♘f3	♘d5

31	cxd6	♖ad8
32	h3	♕f4
33	♕c1	♕xd6

Black has rounded up the white pawn and now White has weak pawns on d4 and b4 as well as a draughty king position.

34	♖c6	♕g3
35	♖c2	♘f4
36	♔f1	

White has been struggling to hold on, but the weak squares in his position will eventually tell.

36	...	h6
37	♖e3	♘d5

38	♖b3	f5

To establish a rook on e4.

39	♔g1	♔h7
40	♕b1	♘f4
41	h4	

Instead 41 ♘e5 ♕g5 42 ♘f7 ♕h4 43 g3 ♘xh3+ 44 ♔h2 ♕h5 45 ♘xd8 ♘f4+ 46 ♔g1 ♘e2+ 47 ♔g2 ♘xd4 wins for Black.

41	...	♕g4
42	♕f1	♘e6
43	d5	♘d4
44	♘xd4	♕xd4+

The white queen's pawn now falls to Black's major pieces and White still has to defend his king.

45	♕f2	♕d1+
46	♔h2	♖xd5
47	♖f3	♖e1

48	g3	

If 48 ♖xf5 ♖h1+ 49 ♔g3 ♕d3+ 50 ♖f3 ♕g6+ 51 ♔f4 ♖d4+ 52 ♕xd4 ♖xh4+ 53 ♔e3 ♖xd4 54 ♔xd4 ♕xc2 wins for Black.

48	...	♖de5
49	♖d2	♕b1
50	♖b2	♕e4

Now White can hardly move

any of his pieces. The rook on f3 cannot move because of mate on h1, and the rook on b2 must remain on the second rank to prevent ... ♖e2.

51	♕g2	♕d5
52	♖bf2	♖1e4
53	♕f1	♖e1
54	♕g2	♕e6

White's pieces are huddled around his king and he cannot hold out much longer.

55	♕h3	♖1e2
56	♕g2	♖xf2
57	♖xf2	♖e4

Now Black threatens to annex

the b-pawn and 58 ♖b2 ♕e5 is no better than the game.

58	♕f3	♔g6
59	♕a3	♕e5
	0-1	

Black threatens ...♖xh4+ and ...♖e3 and White cannot meet both of these. A fine game by Smyslov after Malich's unincisive opening play.

Perhaps the most critical lines against 4...a5 are those where White fianchettoes his king's bishop, to which we now turn our attention.

Game 43
Kasparov-Yusupov
USSR Championship 1981

1	d4	♘f6
2	c4	e6
3	♘f3	♗b4+
4	♗d2	a5
5	g3	0-0
6	♗g2	b6

White gains nothing by 7 ♘e5; after 7...♖a7 the white knight will soon be driven away by ...d7-d6.

| 7 | 0-0 | ♗a6 |

The natural 7...♗b7 takes play into lines very similar to a Queen's Indian Defence.

| 8 | ♗g5!? | |

An interesting pawn sacrifice. After 8...♗xc4 9 ♘fd2 ♗d5 10 e4 ♗c6 11 e5 h6 12 ♗h4 g5 13 exf6 ♕xf6 White obtains good play. Fearing a prepared variation, Yusupov declines the pawn

and retreats his bishop.

| 8 | ... | ♗e7 |
| 9 | ♕c2 | |

A strong positional move; White prepares to advance in the centre with e4.

| 9 | ... | ♘c6 |

This would be a good move if White rushed in with 10 e4 ♘b4 11 ♕e2 d5 when Black has a good game, but Kasparov's next move simply prevents this and leaves the black knight on c6 misplaced. Yusupov should have played 9...h6 10 ♗xf6 ♗xf6 with the idea of ...d7-d6 and ...♘d7.

10	a3!	h6
11	♗xf6	♗xf6
12	♖d1	♕e7
13	e3!	

Another fine move from Kasparov; 13 e4 e5 14 d5 ♘d4 15 ♘xd4 exd4 is fine for Black, but now 13...e5 14 ♘c3 ♗xc4 15 dxe5 ♗xe5 16 ♘xe5 ♕xe5 17 ♖xd7 leaves White with a big advantage, so Black cannot advance his centre pawns. The best manoeuvre is to reposition his bishop by ...g7-g6 and ...♗g7.

13	...	♖ae8
14	♘fd2	g5

This is a risky move in the long run, since it weakens Black's kingside position, but Yusupov wants to build up a kingside attack by ...♗g7 and ...f7-f5-f4.

15	♘c3	♗g7
16	♘b5	

A good alternative was 16 f4, preventing ...f7-f5 and ...f5-f4.

16	...	♕d8
17	f4	♘e7

The knight comes round to a good post on f5, eyeing the weak white pawn on e3.

18	♘f3	♘f5
19	♕f2	

Kasparov decides to sacrifice a pawn, but it is not clear whether he obtains sufficient compensation; 19 ♕e2 was playable.

19	...	c6
20	♘c3	gxf4
21	gxf4	♗xc4
22	e4	♘d6?!

The knight rather gets in the way here. After 22...♘e7 23 ♔h1 f5 24 e5 White has some compensation for the pawn.

| 23 | ♘e5 | |

Now Black is in some difficulties. After 23...♗a6 24 ♔h1 f5 25 ♖g1 fxe4 26 ♗xe4 White has a strong attack on the kingside.

23	...	f5
24	♘xc4	♘xc4
25	b3	♘d6
26	e5	

The black knight gets kicked around, while White increases his space advantage. 26...♘e4 27 ♗xe4 fxe4 28 ♘xe4 is very bad for Black and 26...♘f7 27 ♗f3 followed by ♔h1, ♖g1 and ♗h5 is also very awkward.

26	...	♘c8
27	♗f3	♔h7

| 28 | ♗h5 | ♖e7 |
| 29 | ♔h1 | ♖g8 |

It is hard to see why this is incorrect; not 29...♗h8 30 ♖g1 ♖g7 31 ♖xg7+ ♗xg7 32 ♖g1 ♕e7 33 ♕g3 ♖g8 34 ♘b1 with the idea of ♘d2-f3-h4.

| 30 | ♖g1 | ♗h8 |

Now comes a real bombshell.

| 31 | ♘e4! |

White threatens to play ♘f6+ winning the game.

| 31 | ... | fxe4 |
| 32 | f5 |

Now White intends f5-f6 winning. If 32...e3 33 ♕c2 wins so Black should play 32...♕f8 33 ♖xg8 ♔xg8 34 f6 ♖g7 35 ♕e2 ♖g5 36 h4 ♗xf6 37 hxg5 ♗xg5 with a clear advantage to White. Probably shell-shocked, Yusupov crumbles.

32	...	♖g5
33	♖xg5	hxg5
34	f6	♔h6
35	fxe7	♕xe7
36	♗f7	d6
37	♖f1	g4

If 37...dxe5 38 ♕e2.

| 38 | ♗xe6 | ♕xe6 |
| 39 | ♕h4+ | 1-0 |

39...♔g7 is met by 40 ♖f6. A very imaginative game by Kasparov.

Black should play solidly in the centre with ...c7-c6 and ...d7-d5 against this set-up rather than with ...♘c6, as in the following game.

Game 54
Serebrjanik-Topalov
Vrnjacka Banja 1991

1	d4	e6
2	♘f3	♘f6
3	c4	♗b4+
4	♗d2	a5
5	g3	b6
6	♗g2	♗a6
7	♕c2	0-0
8	0-0	c6
9	♗f4	♗e7
10	♘bd2	d5
11	b3	♘bd7
12	e4	♖c8
13	e5	♘h5

Although White has an imposing centre, Black's position is solid.

| 14 | ♗e3 | g6 |
| 15 | ♖fd1 | ♘g7 |

16	g4	f5
17	exf6	♗xf6
18	♖ac1	♗e7
19	♕b2	♗d6
20	♘e5	♕e7
21	♖c2	♘xe5
22	dxe5	♗c5
23	♘f1	♗xe3
24	♘xe3	♗b7
25	a3	♖f4

The black rook is well placed here to put pressure on the white pawns.

26	b4	axb4
27	axb4	h5
28	h3	hxg4
29	hxg4	♔h7

Black moves his king to allow him to attack on the kingside.

30	b5	c5

31	cxd5	exd5
32	♗xd5	♖d8

Pinning the bishop, which allows Black to smash the white kingside.

33	f3	♘e6
34	♖cc1	♘g5
35	♔g2	♘xf3

36	♖h1+	♔g7
37	♔g3	

37 e6+ is well met by ...♘d4.

37	...	♖b4
38	♕c3	♘d4
39	♔g2	♖xd5
	0-1	

In conclusion, 4...a5 combined with a fianchetto of the queen's bishop offers Black good chances of equality.

6   4 ♗d2 a5; Black plays ...d7-d5 or ...d7-d6

In this chapter we shall look at 1 d4 ♘f6 2 c4 e6 3 ♘f3 ♗b4+ 4 ♗d2 a5 again but this time consider lines in which Black plays ...d7-d5 or ...d7-d6 at some stage.

The system with ...d7-d5 was popularized by the Russian grandmasters Smyslov and Taimanov in the 1980s, and we have already seen an example in Browne-Smyslov in the Historical Introduction.

Game 55
Reefschläger-Taimanov
USSR 1981

1	d4	♘f6
2	c4	e6
3	g3	♗b4+
4	♗d2	a5
5	♗g2	d5
6	♕c2	♘c6
7	♘f3	

We are now back to the Bogo-

Indian, and Taimanov embarks on his pet manoeuvre to exchange queens.

7	...	dxc4
8	♕xc4	♕d5

Black threatens the white queen which has only one suitable retreat square on d3, after which Black can move his queen to h5 or offer another exchange of queens by ...♕e4. Instead White elects to exchange queens, but in so doing frees the black queen's bishop for action.

9	♕xd5	exd5
10	0-0	

The game Browne-Smyslov in the Historical Introduction continued instead 10 ♘c3 ♗e6 11 ♖c1 a4 with good play for Black.

10	...	♗f5
11	♘c3	♗e4!?

An interesting move, establishing the bishop on the strong e4 square White cannot take the bishop without losing a piece 12 ♘xe4 dxe4 13 ♗xb4 exf3.

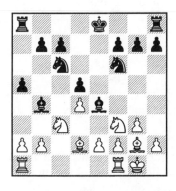

12	♗g5	♗xc3
13	bxc3	♘d7

White has the two bishops, but Black has an equal game since White's queenside pawns are weak.

14	♗h3	h6
15	♗f4	0-0-0

Black could have played 15...♗xf3 16 exf3 0-0-0 when he has the positional plan of ...♔b8 and ...♘b6 when White's queenside is weak. White could then consider sacrificing a pawn to open up the position for his bishops by 17 c4 dxc4 18 ♖fc1 ♘xd4 19 ♔f1.

16	♘d2	♗h7
17	e4!?	

White offers a pawn; after 17...dxe4 18 d5 ♘e7 19 d6 ♘d5 20 dxc7 ♖dg8 21 ♗d6 f5 22 ♘c4 ♘xc7 23 ♘xa5 White will develop a strong attack on the queenside.

17	...	♘e7
18	f3	f5

Black attempts to block off the powerful white bishop on h3.

19	exf5	

Instead 19 e5 ♘f8 followed by ...♘e6 is better for Black, but worth attention is 19 c4! trying to open up the c-file. Black's best continuation is 19...g5 20 ♗e3 dxe4 21 fxe4 g4 22 ♗g2 fxe4 23 ♘xe4 ♘f5 24 ♗f2 with a double-edged position, perhaps slightly better for White.

19	...	♘xf5
20	♖fe1	♖de8
21	g4	

21 ♗g2 and 21 ♗e5 were better.

21	...	g5
22	gxf5	

Or 22 ♗xc7 ♘xd4 23 ♗xa5 ♘c2 24 ♖xe8+ ♖xe8 25 ♖d1 ♘e5 with strong counterplay for Black.

22	...	gxf4
23	f6	♔d8
24	♗xd7?	

24 f7 ♖xe1+ 25 ♖xe1 ♖f8 26 ♗e6 c6 27 c4 should lead to equality.

24	...	♔xd7
25	♖e5	♖xe5
26	dxe5	♔e6

White has two dangerous looking passed pawns, but they are held up by the black king.

27	♖e1	c5
28	c4	d4
29	♔f2	♗c2
30	♘e4	b6
31	♘d2	a4

Black is planning to advance his pawn to a3 to create a target for his bishop on a2.

32	♖c1	♗d3
33	♖e1	a3
34	♖g1	♔xe5
35	♖g7	♔xf6
36	♖b7	♖e8

The winning move; Black threatens to win the white knight by ...♖e2+, and this forces White to exchange rooks.

37	♖xb6+	♖e6
38	♖xe6+	♔xe6
39	♔e1	♔d6
40	♔d1	♔c6
	0-1	

White is powerless to stop the black king invading via b6 and a5.

A more dangerous plan is one in which White does not exchange on d5, as in the next game.

Game 56
Sosonko-Herzog
Lucerne (Olympiad) 1982

1	d4	♘f6
2	c4	e6
3	g3	d5

4	♗g2	♗b4+
5	♗d2	a5
6	♕c2	♘c6

This attack on the d4 point practically forces 7 ♘f3, since 7 e3 e5 opens up the game in Black's favour.

7　♘f3　dxc4
8　♕xc4　♕d5
9　♕d3

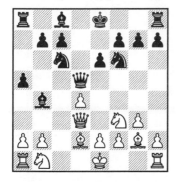

The most challenging move for Black. He could now castle as in Browne-Smyslov, Tilburg 1982, which continued 9...0-0 10 ♘c3 ♕h5 11 ♗f4 ♘d5 12 0-0 ♘xf4 13 gxf4 ♖d8 14 e3 f6 15 ♘e2 ♕f7 16 ♘g3 ♗f8 17 ♖ac1 ♘b4 18 ♕b1 c6 19 a3, when a draw was agreed, but White can improve with 11 a3 ♗d6 (or 11...♗e7 12 0-0 ♖d8 13 ♕c4 ♗d7 14 ♖fe1 with a clear advantage to White) 12 e4 ♖d8 13 ♕c4, as in de Boer-van der Wiel, Arnhem/Amsterdam 1983. It is much safer for Black to force the exchange of queens.

9　...　♕e4
10　♕xe4　♘xe4
11　♗xb4

A good alternative for White is 11 ♗f4 ♗d6 12 e3 with an edge.

11　...　axb4

This opens the a-file for Black's rook. Instead 11...♘xb4 12 ♘a3 is perhaps better for White as he will be able to consolidate after driving away the black knight on e4 by ♘d2.

12　♘bd2

Madsen-Taimanov, Gausdal 1992, went instead 12 0-0 ♗d7 13 ♖d1 ♔e7 14 ♘e5 ♘xe5 15 dxe5 ♘c5 with good play for Black down the a-file.

12　...　♘xd2
13　♔xd2

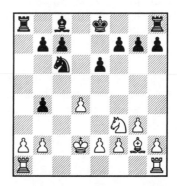

White has the freer position, but Black has counterplay down the a-file.

13　...　♔e7
14　♖hc1　♖d8

Black attempts to pressurise d4, but this is a faulty plan; he should concentrate on the white weakness on a2 with 14...♗d7 15 e3 ♖a7 16 ♘e1 ♖ha8 17 ♘d3 ♖xa2 18 ♖ab1 ♖2a4 19 ♘c5 ♖4a7 20 ♘xb7 ♖xb7 21 ♗xc6 ♗xc6 22 ♖xc6 ♔d7, which led to an equal position in Adamski-

Sydor, Gdynia 1982.

15	e3	e5

Black planned to equalize by this thrust, but he must have underestimated White's next move.

16	♖xc6!	bxc6
17	♘xe5	

White has a pawn for the exchange for a pawn and Black has several weak pawns on the queenside.

17	...	♖d6
18	♘xc6+	♔f8
19	♘xb4	♖b8
20	♘d3	♗a6
21	b3	

Now White has consolidated his position and has three good pawns for the exchange.

21	...	♗xd3
22	♔xd3	c5
23	♖c1	cxd4
24	exd4	♖a6
25	♖c2	♔e7
26	♗d5	

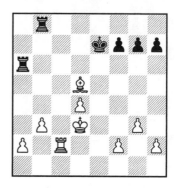

White threatens to play a2-a4 followed by ♗c4 winning, so Black must blockade.

26	...	♖a3
27	♔e4	f6
28	♗c6	

Threatening to trap the black rook by ♗a4.

28	...	♖a6
29	♗a4	

White threatens ♖c7+.

29	...	♔d6
30	♖c5	g6
31	g4	♖b7

This allows White to penetrate to the eighth rank, but otherwise White could have continued with f4-f5 followed by ♖d5+ and ♖d7+.

32	♖c8	♖c7

33	&d8+	&e7
34	&h8	

Black decides that he cannot defend passively by 43...&d6 because White can build up pressure on the kingside by h4-h5-h6.

34	...	&c2
35	&xh7+	&f8
36	f4	&xa2
37	f5	gxf5+
38	gxf5	

White is planning to move his bishop to e6 when he will be able to win the f-pawn with &f7+.

38	...	&d6
39	&b5	&a1
40	d5	&e1+
41	&d4	&e5
42	&c6	

Now White ties up the black rook on d6 ready to capture it later.

42	...	&xf5
43	b4	&g8
44	&a7	&f1
45	&a8+	1-0

Probably the system with ...d7-d5 is too simplistic to promise full equality if White plays accurately.

Black can also play more slowly in the centre with ...d7-d6, preparing a later ...e6-e5 or ...c7-c5.

Game 57
Gligoric-Tal
Belgrade 1968

1	d4	&f6
2	c4	e6
3	&f3	&b4+
4	&d2	a5
5	&c3	

The fianchetto 5 g3 is considered in the next game.

5	...	0-0
6	e3	d6
7	&c2	&bd7
8	a3	

White can try 8 e4 but then Black can equalize with 8...e5.

8	...	&xc3
9	&xc3	&e7
10	&e2	

Again 10 e4 e5 is satisfactory for Black.

10	...	a4

Tal decides to fix an occupation square on b3 rather than move in the centre.

11	0-0	b6
12	♘d2	♗b7
13	e4	c5

Black prefers this to the solid ...e6-e5 aiming to use his bishop on the long white diagonal. Now White cannot play 14 d5 exd5 15 cxd5 because of 15...♘xd5.

| 14 | e5 | ♘e8 |

| 15 | f4 |

15 ♘f3 was worth consideration. Now White is forced into an unfavourable sequence.

15	...	cxd4
16	♗xd4	dxe5
17	fxe5	♘xe5
18	♗xb6	♘d6
19	♗d4	♘f5
20	♗xe5	♕c5+
21	♖f2	♕xe5
22	♘f3	♕c5

The pin on the white rook is murderous.

23	♕c3	♖fd8
24	♕b4	♕a7
25	c5	♖ab8
26	♕c3	♖bc8
27	♖d1

Or 27 ♖c1 ♖d5.

27	...	♖xd1+
28	♗xd1	♖xc5
29	♕b4	♗c6
30	♕f4	♖d5
31	♗e2	h6
32	♘e5	♗a8
33	g4	g5
34	♕c4	♖xe5
	0-1	

Play takes on a more critical nature if Black plays an early ...e6-e5 rather than delaying action in the centre.

Game 58
Shirov-Korchnoi
Wijk aan Zee 1993

| 1 | d4 | ♘f6 | | 2 | c4 | e6 |

3	♘f3	♗b4+
4	♗d2	a5
5	g3	d6
6	♗g2	♘bd7
7	0-0	e5
8	♘c3	

8	...	exd4

Black does not need to exchange on d4, but he wishes to obtain free play for his pieces; he might also try 8...0-0 9 ♕c2 ♖e8 10 e4 c6 11 ♖fe1 ♕c7 12 b3, with a slight advantage to White, as in M. Kovacs-Gipslis, Lublin 1969.

9	♘xd4	0-0
10	♕c2	♘b6
11	b3	

In his notes to the game Shirov suggests 11 ♖ad1! ♘xc4 12 ♗g5 with excellent play for the pawn.

11	...	♗c5
12	♘f5	

12 e3, maintaining the tension, is also quite good.

12	...	♖e8
13	♖ad1	a4
14	♗c1!	axb3
15	axb3	♖e5

16	e4	♗xf5
17	exf5	c6
18	♗f4	♖e8
19	♗g5!	h6
20	♗h4	

Not 20 ♗xf6 ♕xf6 21 ♘e4 ♕xf5 winning a pawn.

20	...	♘bd7
21	♘e4	♕c7
22	♘xc5?	

White should have exchanged on f6: 22 ♘xf6+ ♘xf6 23 ♗xf6 gxf6 24 ♕d2 ♔g7 25 b4 with a clear advantage .

22	...	dxc5
23	h3	♖a3!
24	g4	♕a5
25	♗g3?	

A bad mistake; 25 ♖d2! would have retained a slight advantage for White according to Shirov.

25	...	♖a2
26	♕d3	♘e5
27	♕b1	♖e2

28	f4??	

Necessary was 28 ♕a1 ♖a2 29 ♕b1 repeating moves - Shirov.

28	...	♕c3
29	♗h4	

White cannot play either 29 fxe5 ♕xg3; or 29 ♗e1 ♕e3+ 30 ♗f2 (not 30 ♔h1 ♘eg4 31 hxg4 ♘xg4 winning for Black) 30...♘f3+ 31 ♗xf3 ♕xf3 32 ♖d3 ♕xf4 with good play for Black.

29	...	♖b2!
30	♕c1	♖c2
31	♕b1	

If 31 fxe5 ♖xc1 32 ♖xc1 ♕e3+ is good for Black.

31	...	♖b2
32	♕c1	♖c2
33	♕b1	♘d3
34	♖f3	♖ee2
35	♖fxd3	♖xg2+
36	♔f1	♖h2
37	♔g1	♖cg2+
38	♔f1	♖b2
39	♔g1	♖bg2+
40	♔f1	♖b2
41	♔g1	♕a5 *(D)*
42	♕xb2	

Or 42 ♕c1 ♖bg2+ 43 ♔f1 ♕a2.

42	...	♖xb2
43	g5	♕a2
	0-1	

In conclusion, the plan of ...d7-d6 and ...e6-e5, while playable, is probably not quite sufficient for full equality.

7 4 ♗d2 c5

In the first edition of this book, published in 1985, the system with 4...c5 barely received a mention, but it has since become one of Black's main defences against 4 ♗d2. White is left with a difficult choice as to whether or not he should capture on b4.

Game 59
Alexandria-Jackson
Lucerne (Olympiad) 1982

1	d4	♘f6
2	c4	e6
3	♘f3	♗b4+
4	♗d2	c5
5	♗xb4	cxb4
6	g3	

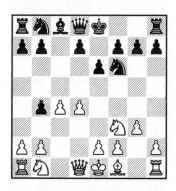

Although the pawn on b4 prevents White from developing his knight on c3, Black cannot exert as much pressure on the white centre as with a pawn on c7; Black usually has to play for ...e6-e5.

6	...	b6
7	♗g2	♗b7
8	0-0	0-0

An interesting alternative, popularised by the Bulgarian grandmaster Kiril Georgiev, is 8...a5 9 a3 ♘a6, supporting the outpost on b4 and preventing the white knight from coming to c3. The game Gligoric-Georgiev, Sarajevo 1986, continued 10 ♘bd2 0-0 11 ♖e1 d6 12 e4 ♘d7 with dynamic play.

9	a3	

The slightly passive 9 ♘bd2 was considered in the game Adorjan-Salov in the Historical Introduction.

9	...	♕e7

It is probably futile now to attempt to hold the outpost on b4. The immediate 9...bxa3 10 ♖xa3 (10 ♘xa3 d6, followed by ...♘bd7 and ...e6-e5, gives good chances of equality) 10...♘c6 11 ♘c3 leaves White with only a slight advantage.

10   ♕a4

Now Black could try to hold onto her outpost by 10...a5, but after 11 ♕b3 ♘c6 12 d5 exd5 13 cxd5 ♘b8 14 ♘d4 White has a big advantage.

10	...	bxa3
11	♘xa3	d6
12	♖fe1	

White has a development advantage and pressure down the half-open a-file. Black could now play 12...♘bd7 13 ♘b5 a6 14 ♘c3 but White would retain the advantage because of the weakness of the black b-pawn.

12	...	♘c6
13	e4	e5
14	d5	♘b8

Black hopes to be able to post a knight on the c5 square which she could do if she played ...a7-

a5, but then a white knight would obtain a fine square on b5 aiming at the d6 pawn.

15   ♘b5   a6

After 15...a5? 16 ♕a3 ♖d8 17 ♘h4 g6 18 f4 White has a big advantage since Black cannot capture on f4 because of e5.

16	♘c3	♕c7
17	♘d2	♘bd7
18	♕a3	♖ac8
19	♗h3	

A useful move since it restricts the knight on d7.

19	...	♕c5
20	b4	♕d4
21	♖ed1	

White is threatening to win the black queen with ♘e2, so Black must provide an escape route.

21   ...   b5

The only move; 21...a5 22 ♘e2 axb4 23 ♕a7 wins for White.

| 22 | ♘e2 | ♕b6 |
| 23 | cxb5 | axb5 |

Not 23...♕xb5 24 ♘c3 ♕d3 25 ♖ac1 with the threat of ♗f1 winning the queen.

| 24 | ♕a7 | ♖c7 |

25   ♘c1!

This fine move prepares the transfer of the knight to a5 via b3 or to d3.

25	...	♖a8
26	♕xb6	♘xb6
27	♖xa8+	♘xa8
28	f4!	

The black queen's knight has been deflected to a8, and the other knight cannot defend e5 from d7, so White forces her op-ponent to exchange on f4; if 28...♘b6 29 fxe5 dxe5 30 ♘d3 ♘bd7 31 ♘b3 and White threatens ♘bc5 with a clear advantage.

28	...	exf4
29	gxf4	♘b6
30	♘cb3	

White threatens 31 ♘d4 win-ning the b-pawn; 30...♘c4 31 ♘xc4 bxc4 32 ♘a5 ♗a6 33 e5 ♘e4 34 ♗f5 wins for White.

30	...	♖c3
31	♗g2	♗c8
32	♖a1	g6
33	♖a5	♗d7
34	♖a6	♘c8
35	e5	♘h5
36	exd6	♘xf4
37	♘c5	1-0

After 37...♖c2 38 ♘xd7 ♖xd2 39 ♘f6+ ♔h8 40 d7 is decisive.

In the next game Black incau-tiously allows his opponent to advance in the centre.

Game 60
Portisch-Hjartarson
Reykjavik 1988

1	d4	♘f6
2	c4	e6
3	♘f3	♗b4+
4	♗d2	c5
5	♗xb4	cxb4
6	g3	0-0
7	♗g2	d6
8	♘bd2	♕c7

Either 8...♘c6 or 8...♖e8 would be more accurate than this move, which commits the queen prematurely.

9	0-0	b6?!

This allows White to break in the centre. Instead 9...e5?! 10 c5! exd4 11 cxd6 ♕xd6 12 ♘c4 is also good for White; but worthy of consideration are 9...a5 and 9...♘fd7!?.

10	d5	

Also good for White was 10 a3! bxa3 11 ♖xa3 ♗b7 12 b4

with a space advantage on the queenside.

10   ...   ♗b7

Not 10...e5?? 11 ♘xe5 winning a pawn; Black is unable to recapture the knight because of 12 d6 spearing the black rook on a8.

11   dxe6   fxe6

Black now has weak pawns on d6 and e6 which White can try and exploit.

12   ♘d4

The direct 12 ♗h3 e5 (12...♖e8!?) 13 ♕b3 ♘c6 14 c5+ d5 leaves Black with a strong centre; best was 12 ♘g5 ♗xg2 13 ♔xg2 ♕e7 14 ♘de4 h6 (14...♘e8 15 ♕d3 with an attack) 15 ♘xf6+ ♕xf6 16 ♘f3 when White has the edge because of the weakness of the black pawns on d6 and e6 (Ftacnik).

12	...	♗xg2
13	♔xg2	e5!
14	♘f5	♘c6
15	♘f3	─♖ad8
16	♘e3	♔h8
17	♖c1?!	

17 ♘d5 ♕b7 18 ♘xf6 gxf6

was better since Black has less control over the central light squares.

17	...	♕b7
18	♘d5	♘e4!
19	♕c2	♘c5

Although Black still has a weakness on d6, he has pressure down the long white diagonal and can play to undermine the white knight on d5.

20   ♘g5

White should be careful of the undermining of his knight on d5. Better was 20 h4 b5 with equality as now White is driven back.

| 20 | ... | g6 |
| 21 | ♕d2 | |

Instead 21 e3 b5! underlines the fragility of White's position.

| 21 | ... | b5 |
| 22 | f3 | b3! |

This fine move establishes an outpost on c2 as White's reply is forced.

| 23 | a3 | ♘d4 |
| 24 | e4 | |

It is natural for White to want to keep an outpost for his knight on d5, but this leads to a weakness on f3. 24 e3? was bad because of 24...bxc4! 25 ♘b4 ♘c2 26 ♘xc2 bxc2 27 ♖xc2 d5 when Black has a large advantage with his massive pawn centre; but 24 ♘e3! bxc4 25 ♖xc4 h6 26 ♘h3 g5 leaves Black only slightly better because the black centre pawns must stay defending the black knights.

24	...	bxc4
25	♖xc4	h6!
26	♘h3	g5

Black fixes the weakness on f3.

| 27 | ♖c3 |

More circumspect was 27 ♖cc1 ♕h7.

27	...	♕f7
28	♕e3	♕g6
29	♘e7	♕h7
30	♘d5	♖f7
31	♘g1	♖df8

Black could have played 31...♘c2! 32 ♕e2 ♖df8 with a big advantage.

| 32 | ♖cc1 | ♕g6 |

Instead 32...g4 33 fxg4 ♘c2 34 ♕e2 ♕xe4+ gives Black a slightly better endgame.

33	♘c3	h5
34	♖f2	♘ce6
35	♖cf1	h4
36	g4	♘f4+ (D)
37	♔h1	♖c8

37...♕e6 maintains the pressure.

| 38 | ♖d1 | ♕e6 |
| 39 | ♖fd2 | ♖c6 |

This allows White to leap out; 39...♕f6 was good.

| 40 | ♘d5! | ♖c2 |

Not 40...♘xd5? 41 exd5 ♕xd5 42 ♕xg5 when White crashes through on the kingside.

| 41 | ♘xf4 | gxf4 |

After 41...♖xf4 42 ♘e2 ♖xd2 43 ♕xd2 ♖xf3 (or 43...♘xe2 44 ♕xe2 with equality) 44 ♘xd4 exd4 45 ♕xd4+ ♕f6 the endgame is equal.

42	♕f2	♖h7
43	♘e2	♖xd2
44	♖xd2	♕c4
45	♘xf4?

This gives Black another chance. He could not play 45 ♘xd4? ♕c1+ winning because of ...h4-h3+, or 45 ♘c3 h3 which is also good for Black; but 45 h3! ♘xe2 46 ♖xe2 was the correct continuation for White

| 45 | ... | ♕c1+ |
| 46 | ♔g2 | ♔g8 |

Black misses a chance; correct was 46...h3+! 47 ♘xh3 ♘xf3! and now 48 ♖e2 is the best move: 48...♖f7 (not 48...♖xh3? 49 ♔xh3 ♘g1+ 50 ♔g2 ♘xe2 51 ♕xe2 ♕c2 52 ♔f3 ♔g7 with an edge for White) 49 ♖e3 (or 49 ♕e3

♘h4+ 50 ♔g3 ♖f3+) 49...♘g5 50 ♕e2 (or 50 ♕h4+ ♘h7 51 ♖f3 ♕xb2+ 52 ♘f2 ♖xf3 53 ♔xf3 ♕c3+ 54 ♔g2 ♕c7 with a big advantage for Black) 50...♗c7 with dangerous threats (Ftacnik).

47   ♘d5!

Not 47 ♘d3? h3+ 48 ♔g3 ♕c7 49 f4 ♕e7 50 g5 ♘e6 with an attack; nor 47 ♘h3? ♘xf3.

47   ...   ♖f7??

Black had to play 47...h3+ 48 ♔g3 ♖f7 which is unclear.

48	f4!	♘e6
49	f5	♘g5
50	♖e2!	

Not 50 ♘c3? h3+ 51 ♔g3 ♕xc3+.

50	...	♕c4
51	♕e3	♔f8
52	h3	♖g7
53	♘c3	a5
54	♖d2	♕c6
55	♕d3	♖d7
56	♕e3	♖g7
57	♖f2	♕c4
58	f6	♖g6
59	♕b6	1-0

Often White tries to remove the thorn in his side immediately with an early a2-a3.

Game 61
Beliavsky-Salov
Szirak (Interzonal) 1987

1	d4	♘f6
2	c4	e6
3	♘f3	♗b4+
4	♗d2	c5
5	♗xb4	cxb4
6	a3	

7	♘xa3	

Subsequently the recapture with the rook has become more popular (see the next game).

7	...	0-0
8	e3	♘c6
9	♗e2	b6

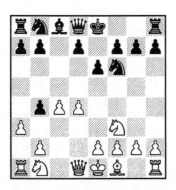

6   ...   bxa3

10	0-0	d6
11	♕b1	

This places the queen offside; 11 ♘c2 was better with the same intention of playing b4, with equal chances.

11	...	a5
12	♖d1	

After 12 ♘c2 e5! 13 b4 ♗f5 the white knight is awkwardly pinned.

12	...	♗a6
13	♘c2	d5

The pin on the c4 pawn gives Black a slight initiative and he uses this to build up a strong position on the kingside.

14	b3	♘e4
15	♕b2	f5
16	g3	

This weakens the kingside light squares; 16 ♗d3 was a better try.

16	...	g5
17	♘e5	♘xe5
18	dxe5	♕c7

Black plays against the weak pawn on e5.

19	♘a3	dxc4
20	♗xc4	♗xc4

21	♘xc4	g4

Black fixes the weak points on f3 and h3.

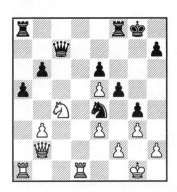

If White had now played 22 ♘d6 ♘g5 23 ♖ac1 ♕g7 then he has difficulties in defending the e5 point against the threat of ...♘f3. Also 22 ♕d4 b5 23 ♕b6 ♕xb6 24 ♘xb6 ♖a6 25 ♘d7 ♖c8 gives Black a clear advantage, since the white knight is badly placed.

22	h4	gxh3
23	♔h2	♕g7
24	♖e1	

Instead 24 ♘xb6 ♖ad8 gives a strong attack.

24	...	♕g4

Not the aggressive 24...f4? 25 exf4 ♖xf4 26 ♖xe4! (26 ♖e2? ♖af8 27 ♖f1 ♘xg3 28 ♖g1 ♘xe2 29 ♖xg7+ ♔xg7 wins) 26...♖xe4 27 f3! when White is perfectly okay.

25	♕e2	♖ad8
26	♘d6	♘g5
27	♖a4	♕xe2

After 27...♕f3 28 ♕f1! is adequate.

28	♖xe2	♘f3+
29	♔h1	♘xe5

Black's pressure on the king-side has forced White to jettison the e-pawn.

30	♖d4	♘f3
31	♖d3	♖d7
32	e4	♘e5
33	♖d1	f4

Black plays carefully to prevent his opponent generating any counterplay; not 33...♖fd8? 34 exf5 ♘f3 35 ♖e3!.

34	gxf4	♖xf4
35	♖c2	♖xe4
36	f3	

If 36 ♖g1+ ♖g4 is sufficient.

36	...	♘xf3
37	♖g1+	

After 37 ♖c8+ ♔g7 38 ♘f5+ ♔f6 39 ♖f8+ ♔e5 40 ♖xd7 ♖e1 is checkmate.

37	...	♘xg1
38	♘xe4	♖d1
39	♔h2	♖e1
40	♖c8+	♔g7
41	♘d6	♘f3+

0-1

A fine game by Salov, and one which serves to highlight Black's chances in the 4...c5 system.

A better strategy for White is to recapture on move seven with the rook, allowing the white knight to go to c3 to fight for control of the central light squares.

Game 62
Petursson-Korchnoi
Reykjavik 1987

1	d4	♘f6
2	c4	e6
3	♘f3	♗b4+
4	♗d2	c5
5	♗xb4	cxb4
6	a3	bxa3
7	♖xa3	*(D)*
7	...	0-0
8	e3	b6

Black fianchettoes his bishop

and waits for White to declare his intentions. Also perfectly acceptable is 8...d6 9 ♗e2 ♘c6 10 ♘c3 e5 11 0-0 ♗g4 with excellent chances of equality.

9	♗d3	♗b7
10	♘c3	d6
11	♕b1	

White plans to gain space on the queenside with b4, which

Black must prevent.

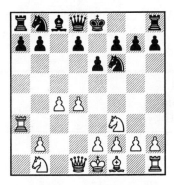

11	...	a5
12	b4	axb4
13	♖xa8	♗xa8
14	♕xb4	

Although Black has a weakness on b6 he is now able to break out in the centre due to the unprotected white bishop on d3.

14	...	e5
15	d5	♘a6
16	♕b1	♘c5

The black knight has a fine post on this square, which fully compensates for the weakness of the b-pawn.

17	♗c2	♗b7
18	0-0	♗a6
19	♘d2	♕c7
20	♕b4	g6
21	♖a1	♖c8
22	g3	♖a8
23	♖b1	♘fd7
24	♖a1	f5
25	♖a3	♖c8
26	♘a4	e4
27	♘xc5	♕xc5
28	♕xc5	♘xc5

Black relies on his knight for active play.

29	♗a4	♔f7
30	♗c6	♖c7
31	♖a1	♗b7
32	♖a7	♖e7
33	♗xb7	♖xb7
34	♖xb7+	♘xb7

A pure knight endgame has been reached in which Black has the advantage. White tries to create some space on the kingside but the black king races up the board.

35	g4	♔f6
36	gxf5	♔xf5
37	♔g2	g5
38	h3	♘c5
39	f3	h5
40	fxe4+	♘xe4
41	♘b3	g4
42	♘d4+	♔g5
43	hxg4	♔xg4
44	♘f3	♘g5
45	♘h2+	♔f5
46	♔g3	♔e4
47	♘f1	♔d3
48	♔h4	♘e4
49	♔xh5	♔xc4

50	♔g4	b5
51	♔f4	♔d3
	0-1	

Another fine demonstration of

Black's strategy by Korchnoi.

White can also delay the capture on b4 and fianchetto his king's bishop.

Game 63
Hommeles-Blees
Netherlands 1987

1	d4	♘f6
2	c4	e6
3	♘f3	♗b4+
4	♗d2	c5
5	g3	b6

Here 5... ♕b6 is a major alternative (see the next game, Vaisman-Wirthensohn).

| 6 | ♗g2 | ♗b7 |
| 7 | d5 | |

White sacrifices a pawn to disrupt his opponent's development, but Black should be able to consolidate with accurate play. Of course 7 ♗xb4 cxb4 or 7 0-0 0-0 8 ♗xb4 cxb4 simply transposes to positions considered earlier.

| 7 | ... | exd5 |

8	♗xb4	cxb4
9	♘h4	♕c7
10	cxd5	♕e5
11	♘d2	♗xd5
12	e4	♗e6
13	0-0	♘c6
14	f4	♕xb2
15	f5	♗xa2

Black is three pawns ahead but dangerously behind in development

| 16 | e5 | ♘d5 |

17	f6	♘e3
18	fxg7	♖g8
19	♕e2	♘xg2
20	♕xg2	♕d4+
21	♔h1	♗e6
22	♘e4	0-0-0

23	♘d6+	♚b8
24	♖xa7	

24	...	♗d5
25	♘f3	♘xa7
26	♘xd4	♗xg2+
27	♚xg2	♖xg7
28	♖a1	♖g4
29	♘b3	♘c6
30	♖a6	♘xe5
31	♖xb6+	♚c7
32	♖a6	♖b8
33	♘a5	♘c6
34	♘ac4	b3
35	♖a1	♖d4
	0-1	

Black is not able to capture the rook immediately but can simplify to an ending.

Black can also head for immediate complications with 5...♕b6, which was popularized by Korchnoi.

Game 64
Vaisman-Wirthensohn
France-Switzerland 1987

1	d4	♘f6
2	♘f3	e6
3	c4	♗b4+
4	♗d2	c5
5	g3	♕b6

This aggressive move puts pressure on the white queenside but neglects developing the kingside.

6 ♗g2

The immediate pawn sacrifice does not present as many problems; Shvidler-Korchnoi, Beersheva 1987, continued 6 d5 exd5 7 cxd5 ♘xd5 8 ♗g2 ♘f6 9 0-0 d5 10 ♗g5 0-0 11 ♘c3 ♗xc3 12 bxc3 ♘bd7 with advantage to Black.

6 ... ♘c6
7 d5

White sacrifices a pawn to retain the initiative; the alternative is 7 ♕b3.

7	...	exd5
8	cxd5	♘xd5
9	0-0	♘de7
10	e4	

This saddles Black with a backward d-pawn and gives White positional compensation for his material deficit.

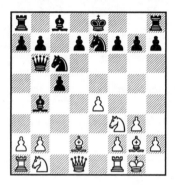

10	...	d6
11	♗e3	♕c7
12	a3	♗a5
13	♘bd2!?	

An interesting alternative to 13 ♗f4 which was played by Kasparov against Korchnoi at Brussels in 1986 (see the Historical Introduction). Kasparov also considers 13 e5!? ♘xe5 14 ♘xe5 dxe5 15 b4 cxb4 16 axb4 ♗b6 17 ♘c3 0-0 18 ♘b5 ♕b8 19 ♗xb6 axb6 20 ♖xa8 ♕xa8 21 ♕d6 with unclear chances.

| 13 | ... | ♗xd2 |

Instead 13...♗e6 14 ♘g5 is awkward for Black since White threatens to capture on e6 and then play ♕b3 or ♕g4; and 13...♗g4 14 ♖c1 also gives White good play down the c-file.

| 14 | ♕xd2 | 0-0 |

This gives up the d-pawn, but after 14...♗g4 15 b4! White has good play for the pawn with his two bishops.

15	♖fd1	♖d8
16	♗f4	♗g4
17	♗xd6	♕c8
18	♕g5	

18 ♕c1 b6 19 e5 ♘f5 20 b4 also leaves White with the initiative.

| 18 | ... | ♕e6 |

After 18...♘g6 19 ♖d5 keeps an edge for White, but not 19 ♗xc5 ♖xd1+ 20 ♖xd1 ♘ce5 with a winning position for Black.

| 19 | ♗xc5 | ♖xd1+ |
| 20 | ♖xd1 | ♘g6? |

Here 20...♕b3 was better, but after 21 ♖e1!? (21 ♖d2 ♗xf3 22 ♗xe7 h6! 23 ♕c5 ♖e8 is good for Black) 21...♗xf3 22 ♗xe7 White has a slight advantage.

| 21 | ♕e3! | ♘ge5 |
| 22 | ♖d5 | ♗xf3 |

Instead 22...♘c4 23 ♕c1 ♕xe4 24 ♘e5 wins.

| 23 | ♗xf3 | ♘xf3+ |

24	♕xf3	♖e8
25	b4	a6
26	♕f5	♕xf5

Here 26...♕xe4 27 ♕xe4 ♖xe4
28 ♖d7 is good for White.

27	exf5	♖d8

Or 27...f6 28 ♖d7 b5 29 ♖c7.

28	♖xd8+	♘xd8
29	♔g2	f6
30	♔f3	♔f7
31	♔e4	♔e8
32	♔d5	♔d7
33	g4	♘f7
34	f4	g5

35	fxg6	hxg6
36	♗d4	♔e7
37	♔c5	♘d8
38	♔b6	f5
39	gxf5	gxf5
40	h4	1-0

In recent games White has sought to neutralize Black's queen's bishop by ♗e2-f3 whilst manoeuvring his knight via e1 to d3 to attack the black pawn on b4.

Game 65
Piket-Schmittdiel
Wijk aan Zee 1993

1	d4	e6
2	c4	♘f6
3	♘f3	♗b4+
4	♗d2	c5
5	♗xb4	cxb4
6	e3	d6
7	♗e2	0-0
8	0-0	b6

Of course 8...♘c6 is perfectly playable, intending to develop the bishop at d7.

9	♘bd2	♗b7
10	♘e1	e5

Kramnik-Kosten, a rapid game at Oviedo 1992, went 10...♕e7 11 ♘d3 a5 12 a3 bxa3 13 bxa3 ♘bd7 14 ♗f3 ♖ab8 with an edge for White.

11	♘d3	exd4
12	exd4	a5
13	a3	bxa3
14	bxa3	

White has a positional advantage due to the weakness of the black pawn on b6.

14	...	♘c6
15	♘f3	♖e8
16	♖e1	♖b8
17	♖c1	♖e4
18	♗f1	♘e7
19	d5	♘f5

20	♕d2	♘d4
21	♘xd4	♖xd4
22	♕b2	♖e4
23	♖xe4	♘xe4
24	♖e1	♘f6
25	♘c1	♗a6
26	♘b3	b5
27	♕d2	bxc4
28	♘xa5	

The white knight heads for the c6 square.

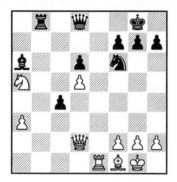

28	...	♖a8
29	♘c6	♕d7
30	♕d4	♗b7
31	♖e7	♕c8
32	♗xc4	♔f8
33	♕e3	♘g8
34	h3	♘xe7
35	♕xe7+	♔g8
36	♕xd6	♗xc6

37	dxc6

White has two pawns for the exchange and pressure against the f7 pawn.

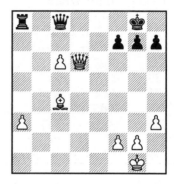

37 ... ♕d8 38 ♕e5 ♕f6 39 ♕c7 ♖e8 40 a4 ♕e7 41 ♕f4 ♖c8 42 a5 ♕e1+ 43 ♔h2 ♕xa5 44 ♕xf7+ ♔h8 45 ♗d5 ♕d8 46 ♕e6 ♕c7+ 47 g3 ♖f8 48 ♔g2 ♕b6 49 ♗f3 ♕c5 50 h4 g6 51 ♕d7 ♕c3 52 ♕d5 ♖f5 53 ♕d8+ ♔g7 54 ♗e4 ♖f7 55 ♕d5 ♕b2 56 ♕c5 ♕e2 57 ♕d4+ ♔h6 58 ♗d5 ♖f8 59 c7 1-0.

As we have seen, the development of the 4...c5 variation in the 1980s owes much to Viktor Korchnoi so it is fitting to end this chapter with another of his games.

Game 66
Kraidman-Korchnoi
Jerusalem 1986

1	d4	♘f6
2	c4	e6
3	♘f3	♗b4+

4	♗d2	c5
5	e3	

A quiet move which is not bad if

White exchanges on b4 rather than transposing to a passive variation of the Nimzo-Indian with 6 ♘c3.

5 ... 0-0

Black can also fianchetto his queen's bishop, as in Stokstad-Renman, Copenhagen 1991: 5...b6 6 ≜d3 ≜b7 7 ≜xb4 cxb4 8 ♘bd2 0-0 9 0-0 d6 10 ♕c2 ♘bd7 11 ♘g5 h6 12 ♘ge4 ♕e7 13 ♖ac1 ♖ac8 with satisfactory play.

6 ♘c3

This does not trouble Black.

6	...	cxd4
7	♘xd4	d5
8	cxd5	exd5

Although Black has an isolated queen's pawn he has active play for his pieces, while the white bishop on d2 is passively placed.

9	≜e2	♘c6
10	♘xc6	bxc6
11	0-0	≜d6

Black repositions his king's bishop to aim at the white king position.

12	♖c1	♕e7
13	♕a4	♖b8
14	♕xc6	♖xb2
15	♘xd5	♘xd5
16	♕xd5	♖d8

Black now has the threat of ...≜xh2+, and White is also threatened with ...♖xd2 followed by ...≜xh2+. He now plays a move which appears good at first sight, but meets with catastrophe.

17	≜a5	≜xh2+
18	♔xh2	♖xd5 *(D)*
	0-1	

After 19 ♖xc8+ ♕f8 20 ♖xf8+ ♔xf8 White will lose a bishop and end up the exchange down.

The 4...c5 line is Black's most

ambitious try against 4 ♗d2, and
has been the subject of hundreds
of grandmaster games over the
past decade. Although White has
now developed some promising
ways of handling this variation it
is clearly an ideal choice for club
and tournament play.

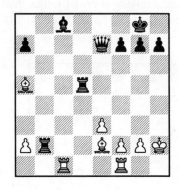

8 4 ♗d2; Black exchanges on d2

Until recently both the immediate exchange 4...♗xd2+ and the delayed exchange 4...♕e7 5 g3 0-0 6 ♗g2 ♗xd2+ were frowned upon by theory as White can recapture with the queen and then develop his knight on c3, but in the past few years Ulf Andersson and several other grandmasters have shown them to be playable. However, White should be able to obtain a slight advantage.

Game 67
Alekhine-Bogolyubov
Budapest 1921

1	d4	♘f6
2	♘f3	e6
3	c4	♗b4+
4	♗d2	♗xd2+
5	♕xd2	d5

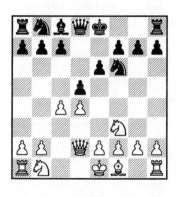

6   e3

Also promising for White is a kingside fianchetto with 6 g3 0-0

7 ♗g2.

6	...	0-0
7	♘c3	♘bd7
8	♗d3	

More accurate is 8 ♖c1, waiting for Black to declare his intentions.

8   ...   c6

This is rather passive but Bogolyubov has a specific idea in mind.

9	0-0	dxc4
10	♗xc4	e5 *(D)*
11	♗b3	

If White recaptures on e5 with the knight then Black can recapture, exploiting the position of the white queen: 11 dxe5 ♘xe5 12 ♕xd8 ♘xf3+ 13 gxf3 ♖xd8 with advantage to Black

11   ...   ♕e7

12	e4	exd4
13	♘xd4	♘c5
14	♗c2	♖d8
15	♖ad1	♗g4
16	f3	♘e6
17	♕f2	♘xd4
18	♖xd4	♗e6
19	♖fd1	b6
20	h3	c5
21	♖4d2	

White has a positional advantage due to his potential control of the d-file and it is difficult for Black to find a safe position for his minor pieces because of the advance of the white kingside pawns.

21	...	♖xd2
22	♕xd2	c4

23	f4	g6
24	♕d4	♖c8
25	g4	

Black is getting squashed so he decides to sacrifice a piece, but this is easily refuted by Alekhine.

25	...	♗xg4
26	hxg4	♘xg4
27	♔g2	

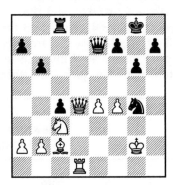

27	...	h5
28	♘d5	♕h4
29	♖h1	♕d8
30	♗d1	1-0

Black was too passive in this game, but this line is hard to play for Black. One of the few players to have mastered the Black side is the Swedish grandmaster Ulf Andersson.

Game 68
Nikolic-Andersson
Niksic 1983

1	d4	♘f6
2	c4	e6
3	♘f3	♗b4+

4	♗d2	♗xd2+
5	♕xd2	0-0
6	♘c3	d5

The position is similar to a Queen's Gambit Declined but the exchange of dark-squared bishops should favour White. In fact, Andersson has worked out a system of satisfactory development.

| 7 | e3 | ♕e7 |
| 8 | ♖c1 | |

In a later game between the same two players, Nikolic played 8 a3, intending to place his queen on c2 and to meet 8...♖d8 with 9 ♖d1. That game, played at Wijk aan Zee in 1984, continued 8...♘bd7 9 ♕c2 dxc4 10 ♗xc4 c5 11 0-0 ♘b6 12 ♗a2 (underling the usefulness of 8 a3) 12...cxd4 13 exd4, when White retained a slight advantage.

| 8 | ... | ♖d8 |

Black plans to exploit the position of the white queen on d2 by exchanging on c4 and then playing ...c7-c5.

9	♕c2	dxc4
10	♗xc4	c5
11	0-0	♘c6
12	dxc5	♕xc5
13	♘e4	♕e7

White cannot now play ♗d3 because of ...♘b4, so he must waste a move and this enables Black to complete his development.

14	a3	♗d7
15	♗d3	h6
16	b4	♖ac8
17	♕b2	♗e8

White could try 18 ♘xf6+ ♕xf6 19 ♕xf6 gxf6, but then Black would have enough play similar to the game.

18	♗b1	♘xe4
19	♗xe4	♕f6
20	♕xf6	gxf

Black's kingside pawns are

shattered, but his king is safe in this queenless middlegame. The pawn complex f7, f6 and e6 is useful since it can control many important central squares.

21	h3	f5
22	♗xc6	♗xc6
23	♘d4	♗d7
24	f4	

White has prevented the advance of the black e-pawn, but he cannot hold it up in the long run.

24	...	♔f8
25	♔f2	♔e7
26	♖fd1	f6
27	♘b3	b6
28	♘d4	♖g8
29	b5	

It is difficult to find a good move here, but this allows Black an outpost on c5.

| 29 | ... | ♖c5 |

| 30 | a4 | |

Now if White plays 30 ♖xc5 bxc5 31 ♘c6+ ♗xc6 32 bxc6 ♖d8 33 ♖b1 ♔d6 34 ♖b7 ♔xc6 35 ♖xa7 the black c-pawn is very dangerous.

30	...	♖gc8
31	♖xc5	♖xc5
32	♔e2	e5

The triumphant advance of the black e-pawn enables the black bishop to enter the game with decisive effect.

33	♘f3	♗e6
34	♖a1	♔d6
35	♖a3	♗d5
36	♔d2	♗e4
37	♖c3	exf4
38	♘e1	

After 38 exf4 ♖xc3 39 ♔xc3 ♗xf3 40 gxf3 ♔c5 41 h4 h5 White must give way and let the black king invade.

38	...	♖xc3
39	♔xc3	fxe3
	0-1	

An important line of play, which is very similar to Andersson's plan, is the exchange of bishops on d2 on move 6, followed by setting up a pawn centre with ...d7-d6 and ...e6-e5.

Game 69
Cunningham-Kindermann
Lucerne (Olympiad) 1982

| 1 | d4 | ♘f6 | | 2 | c4 | e6 |

3	♘f3	♗b4+
4	♗d2	♛e7
5	g3	0-0
6	♗g2	♗xd2+
7	♛xd2	d6

The ambitious 7...♘e4 is considered in the next game.

8	♘c3	e5
9	0-0	♖e8

10	e4	a5

The immediate 10...♗g4 is perfectly playable, intending to meet 11 d5 with 11...♗xf3 12 ♗xf3 a5 13 a3 ♘a6, when White stood slightly better in Meduna-Ivkov, Sochi 1983.

11	♖fe1	

Perhaps 11 h3 is more accurate.

11	...	♗g4
12	d5	♘a6

Black has developed satisfactorily, but White has more space.

13	h3	♗d7
14	♖e2	c6
15	dxc6	♗xc6

Although Black has a weak pawn on d6, it is difficult for White to exploit this.

16	♘e1	♘c5

17	♖d1	♖ed8
18	♘c2	b6
19	♛e3	♘e8
20	♘a3	♘c7
21	♖ed2	♖ab8
22	♔h2	h6
23	h4	♘5e6
24	♘c2	b5

Black liquidates his weak b-pawn. Now White decides to block the centre but this leaves Black with the better minor pieces.

25	♘d5	♗xd5
26	cxd5	♘c5
27	♘e1	b4
28	♗f1	♘e8
29	♖c1	

29 f3 was essential.

29	...	♘f6
30	f3	♘cxe4
31	♖dd1	♘c5
32	♗h3	♛b7
33	♛d2	e4
34	f4	♖e8
35	♘g2	♘d3
36	♖c6	♘xd5
37	♖xd6	♖bd8
38	♖xd8	♖xd8

39	♘e3	♕b6
40	♘xd5	♖xd5
41	♗g2	♘xf4
	0-1	

Finally, we look at a treatment for Black that has a great deal in common with the Dutch Defence.

Game 70
Polugayevsky-Ree
Amsterdam 1981

1	d4	♘f6
2	c4	e6
3	♘f3	♗b4+
4	♗d2	♕e7
5	g3	0-0
6	♗g2	♗xd2+
7	♕xd2	♘e4
8	♕c2	f5

We now have a Dutch formation.

9	0-0	d6

Black is threatening to equalize with ...e6-e5 and White must try to stop this.

10	♘h4	

Here 10 ♘e1 would have been better than this provocative continuation; 10 ♘c3 ♘xc3 11 ♕xc3 ♘d7 is also fine for Black.

10	...	g5

Now 11 ♗xe4 gxh4 12 ♗g2 ♘d7 leads to good play for Black; he has possibilities down the g-file.

11	♘f3	♘d7
12	♘e1	♘ef6
13	♘c3	♘g4

Black is planning to gain play on the kingside by attacking h2 with his queen.

14	♘f3	♕g7
15	e4	f4

16	♘b5	fxg3
17	hxg3	

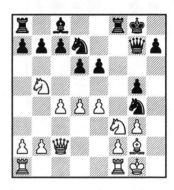

Black has good counterplay because of his pressure on the white king position.

17	...	♘b8
18	e5	

White tries to break through in the centre. Now 18 dxe5 19 ♕e4 h5 20 ♘xe5 ♘xe5 21 dxe5 is good for White.

18	...	a6

So that if 19 ♘c3 dxe5 20 ♕e4 exd4 21 ♘xd4 e5 22 ♕d5+ ♔h8 23 ♘e6 ♕h6 wins for Black

19	♘a3	dxe5
20	♕e4	h5
21	♘xe5	♘xe5
22	♕xe5	

On 22 dxe5 ♘c6 23 f4 ♗d7 Black has good play because of his threat of ...h5-h4 undermining the white pawn chain.

22	...	♛xe5
23	dxe5	♘d7
24	f4	h4!

The thematic break-up of the white pawn chain.

25	♗h3	hxg3
26	♗xe6+	♚g7
27	♖ad1	

This looks awkward for Black because if he plays 27...♘c5 28 ♗xc8 ♖axc8 29 f5 is good for White.

27	...	♘xe5
28	♗xc8	gxf4

Black has two strong passed pawns as compensation for the piece.

| 29 | ♗xb7 | |

This allows the black queen's rook to get into the action; 29 ♖d5 was best.

29	...	♖ab8
30	♗e4	♖xb2
31	♖d5	f3

Black is now threatening ...♖g2+, ...♖h2+ and ...f3-f2+ winning.

32	♘c2	g2
33	♖xe5	gxf1(♛)+
34	♚xf1	♖xa2
35	♚f2	♖f4

Black threatens ...♖xe4 and then ...♖xc2.

36	♗d3	♖xc4
37	♗xc4	♖xc2+
38	♚xf3	♖xc4

Now Black has two extra pawns, but in theory White should be able to draw the endgame. In practice it is a difficult task.

39	♖a5	♖c6
40	♔e4	♔f8
41	♔d5	♖d6+
42	♔c5	♔e7

Black's plan is to place his king on the b7 square, defending the black pawns, and then drive away the white king with the rook.

43	♖a1	♔d7
44	♖h1	♖c6+
45	♔b4	♔c8
46	♔a5	♖b6
47	♖h5	♔b7

Black has protected his pawns and now drives White back.

48	♖g5	♖b1
49	♖h5	♖d1
50	♔b4	♔b6
51	♖h6+	c6

The first stage has been achieved: the white king has been forced back.

52	♖h8	a5+
53	♔c4	♖c1+
54	♔b3	♖g1
55	♖h5	♖d1
56	♔c4	♖c1+
57	♔b3	♖c5

Black drives the white rook off the fifth rank and paves the way for his king to advance.

58	♖h8	♖g5
59	♔c4	♖g4+
60	♔b3	♔b5

61	♖h5+	c5
62	♖h8	a4+
63	♔a3	♖g3+
64	♔b2	♔b4
65	♖b8+	♔c4
66	♖a8	♖g2+
67	♔a3	♔c3 *(D)*
68	♖xa4	

White misses a draw with 68 ♖h8 c4 69 ♖h3+ ♔c2 70 ♔b4

&b2 71 &xc4 a3 72 &b3+ &a2 73 &b8.

| 68 | ... | c4 |
| 69 | &a8 | &g7 |

Now the white rook must stay on the a-file because of mate threats.

70	&a2	&c2
71	&a1	c3
72	&a2	&b7
73	&a6	&d7
74	&a8	&d2

0-1

White cannot stop the pawn: 75 &h8 c2 76 &h2+ &c3 77 &h3+ &d3 78 &h1 &d1 79 &h3+ &d4 followed by marching the king towards the rook via e5, f6 and g7.

So both 4...&xd2+ and 6...&xd2+ are playable, but the positions with ...d7-d5, ...d7-d6 and ...e6-e5 and ...&e4 should all slightly favour White.

9 4 ♗d2 ♕e7 5 g3 ♘c6 6 ♗g2

Before the emergence of the 4...c5 line, Black players almost invariably opted for the solid 4...♕e7 5 g3 ♘c6 variation. Black protects his advanced bishop on b4 and prepares for a later ...d7-d6 and ...e6-e5. In this chapter we look at the immediate 6 ♗g2, and in the next we consider 6 ♘c3. We have already seen several examples of the 6 ♗g2 line in the chapter on positional themes, but here are a couple more.

Game 71
Meduna-Rashkovsky
Lvov 1981

1	d4	♘f6
2	c4	e6
3	♘f3	♗b4+
4	♗d2	♕e7
5	g3	♘c6
6	♗g2	♗xd2+
7	♘bxd2	

Instead 7 ♕xd2 ♘e4 8 ♕c2 ♕b4+ is awkward for White as 9 ♘c3 ♘xc3 10 ♕xc3 ♕xc3+ 11 bxc3 leaves him with doubled pawns and 9 ♘bd2 ♘xd2 10 ♕xd2 ♕xc4 gives insufficient compensation for the sacrificed pawn.

A typical position from this variation. White is ready to advance in the centre with e2-e4 and Black will in turn reply ...d7-d6 and ...e6-e5. It is very likely that White will block the centre with d4-d5 and then aim for a general pawn advance on the queenside. Black's next move is a typical pre-emptive advance.

7	...	a5
8	0-0	d6

9 e4 e5

9...0-0 is considered (by transposition) in the next game, Wedberg-Schneider.

10 d5 ♘b8

The stage is set. White can now obtain queenside play with 11 c5!? 0-0 (after 11...dxc5 12 ♘c4 White has good compensation in view of the threat of d5-d6) 12 cxd6 cxd6 13 a3 a4 14 ♘e1 ♗d7 15 ♘d3 ♗b5 16 ♕f3 ♘a6 17 ♖fc1 ♗xd3 (17...♘d7 was a later improvement in Naumkin-Lisenko, USSR 1983; after 18 ♗h3 ♘dc5 19 ♘xc5 ♘xc5 Black is equal) 18 ♕xd3 ♘c5 19 ♕b5 as in Beliavsky-Rashkovsky, Lvov 1981. In this position Black's knight on c5 is secure, but White has control of the queenside.

11 ♘e1 h5

A very daring move which attempts to deflect White from his strategic plan of a queenside pawn advance. The stereotyped 11...0-0 allows White to establish a slight but sure advantage after

12 ♘d3 ♘a6 13 a3 ♗g4 14 f3 ♗d7 15 b4 axb4 16 axb4 c6 17 dxc6 bxc6 18 ♕b3, as in Yusupov-Petrosian, USSR Championship 1983.

12 ♘c2

Probably best is 12 h4 ♘bd7 13 b3 ♘g4 14 ♕e2 ♘c5 with a satisfactory game for Black.

12 ... h4

Another good example of Black's strategy is West-Oll, Sydney 1991, which continued 12...♗g4 13 ♗f3 ♗h3 14 ♗g2 ♗g4 15 ♗f3 ♗d7 16 ♘e3 ♘a6 17 b3 h4 18 a3 hxg3 19 hxg3 g6 20 ♕c2 ♘h5 21 ♗g2 ♕g5 22 ♘f3 ♕h6 23 ♖fe1 ♘f6 24 ♔f1 ♘c5 25 ♘d2 ♗h3 26 f3 ♘h5 27 ♔f2 ♘xg3 28 ♔xg3 ♕h4+ 29 ♔h2 ♕f2 0-1.

13 ♘e3 g6
14 b3 ♘a6
15 a3 ♔f8

A fine manoeuvre; bringing the king to g7 allows Black to connect his rooks.

16 b4 ♔g7

White cannot capture immediately on a5 since then ...♘c5 would be good for Black.

17 ♘b3 *(D)*

White threatens ♘a5 and if Black exchanges on b4 White obtains pressure down the a-file. Black however, has prepared a pawn sacrifice.

17 ... b6

Now if White captures the pawn 18 bxa5 bxa5 19 ♘xa5 ♘c5 20 ♘c6 ♕e8 21 f3 ♗d7 22 ♘b4 hxg3 23 hxg3 ♘h5 24 ♕e1 ♕e7

Black has the advantage because he threatens ...♕g5 with a further attack on the g-pawn; if White advances with g4 the black knight sinks into f4.

leaves the white e-pawn weak.

23	fxe5	dxe5
24	♕f3	♗xg2
25	♖xg2	axb4
26	axb4	♖h1+
27	♔f2	♘xb4

Black's first material gain.

| 28 | ♘e1 | |

Now Black should continue with 28 ... ♘a6 with the idea of playing the knight to c5.

28	...	♕c5
29	♖gg1	♖1h7
30	♔e2	♕e7
31	♖f2	♖a8
32	♔f1	♘a6

| 18 | ♘c1 | ♗d7 |
| 19 | ♘d3 | ♖h7 |

Black prepares to double rooks, leaving White in a very awkward situation.

20	♖a2	♖ah8
21	f4	hxg3
22	hxg3	♗h3

The exchange of light-squared bishops not only weakens the defences around the white king but

33	♔g2

Best was 33 ♘d3 ♘c5 34 ♘xc5 ♖a1+ 35 ♔g2 ♖xg1+ 36 ♔xg1 bxc5 when Black will obtain the advantage by repositioning his knight on d6 via e8.

33	...	♘c5
34	♖e2	♖ah8
35	♔f1	♘cxe4

36	♘g4	♘xg4
37	♕xg4	♘f6
38	♕g5	♖h5
	0-1	

Instead of meeting e2-e4 with ...e6-e5, Black often allows White the possibility of advancing in the centre with e5.

Game 72
Wedberg-Schneider
Ekjso 1982

1	d4	♘f6
2	c4	e6
3	♘f3	♗b4+
4	♗d2	♕e7
5	g3	♘c6
6	♗g2	♗xd2+
7	♘bxd2	0-0
8	0-0	d6
9	e4	a5

We have seen this pre-emptive move before (see the game Kalantar-Petrosian in the Historical Introduction). It is interesting to see what happens if White

takes up the challenge and advances in the centre with e5. (Note that here 9...e5 is well met by 10 d5 ♘b8 11 b4 a5 12 a3 ♘a6 13 ♕b3, with a slight advantage, as in Korchnoi-Seirawan, Brussels 1988).

10	e5

White can also play 10 d5 (10 0-0 is likely to transpose to positions considered in the previous game) 10...♘b8 11 dxe6 ♗xe6 12 e5 dxe5 13 ♘xe5 c6 with a slight advantage, as in Rivas-Taulbut, Hastings 1982.

10	...	dxe5
11	dxe5	♘d7
12	♖e1	

More normal is 12 ♕e2 ♘c5 13 ♘e4 (or 13 ♖ad1 ♗d7 14 h4 ♖fd8 15 h5 h6 with equality; van der Sterren-Gipslis, Albena 1983) 13...♖d8 14 ♖ad1 ♗d7 15 ♘c3 ♗e8 with a satisfactory game for Black in Sjoberg-Taulbut, Sweden-England 1982.

12	...	♖d8

13	♖e3	♘c5
14	♕e2	♗d7

Although Black is slightly cramped, his pieces have enough scope and hold White's queenside in check. Black can play for a favourable ending since he can gain control of the d-file.

15	h4	♗e8
16	♘e4	♖d7
17	h5	h6

This move is vital. If Black allows White to play h5-h6 then the white knight will settle on f6 with disastrous consequences.

18	g4	♖ad8
19	♘xc5	♕xc5

Black is now threatening favourable exchanges with ...♘d4.

20	♖e4	b6
21	♖f1	♘d4
22	♘xd4	♖xd4
23	♖xd4	♕xd4 (D)

Black has achieved his objective, control of the d-file, and his bishop on e8 will be able to enter the game later via the queenside.

24	♗f3	♕f4
25	♖d1	♖xd1+

26	♕xd1	♕xc4

Not 26...♕xe5 27 ♕d8 ♔f8 28 ♗c6 wins.

27	♕d8	♔f8
28	♔g2	♕c5
29	a3	♕e7
30	♕a8	♕d7

Black plans to unravel with ...♔e7.

31	b4	axb4
32	axb4	♔e7
33	♕b7	♕d8
34	♕e4	♗b5

The bishop has escaped but White still has the initiative.

35	♕h7	♕f8

36	♕c2	♔d8
37	♕d2+	♔c8
38	♕f4	♕e7

Now Black is ready to break with ...f7-f6 but White still has play.

39	♕e4	c6
40	♕h7	♕f8
41	♕e4	f6

Black has to make this break in order to make progress.

42	♕e3	fxe5

If now 43 ♕xe5 ♕f6 44 ♕d6 e5 is good for Black.

43	♕xb6	♕xb4
44	♕a7	e4
45	♕a8+	♔c7
46	♕a7+	♔c8
47	♕a8+	♔c7

Black gains time before advancing his king up the board to escape the checks.

48	♕a7+	♔d6
49	♕b8+	♔d5
50	♕d8+	♕d6
51	♗xe4+	♔c5

The black king has escaped to the white side of the board and the strong position of the black queen will enable the king to escape the checks.

52	♕a8	♕e5
53	♕f8+	♔c4
54	♕f3	♔b4
55	♕e3	

Or 55 ♗xc6 ♗xc6 56 ♕xc6 ♕d5+ 57 ♕xd5 exd5 with a winning king and pawn endgame for Black.

55	...	♕c3
56	♕f4	♕d4
57	♕f8+	c5
58	♗f3	♗c4

Black now plans to exchange the bishops, exposing the white king.

59	♕b8+	♔c3
60	♕g3	♔b2
61	♕b8+	♔c1

The black king has reached a safe haven, and Black will soon be able to advance the c-pawn.

62	♔g3	♗d5
63	♗xd5	exd5
64	♕a7	♕c3+
65	f3	c4
66	♕e7	♔d1

Now White has no more

checks and Black threatens to exchange queens with ...♕e1+.

67	♕d7	♕e1+
68	♔h3	♕h1+
69	♔g3	♕g1+
70	♔h3	♕d4
71	♕a4+	♔e2
	0-1	

White cannot defend the f-pawn except by 72 ♕a3 when ...c4-c3 wins.

White cannot really hope for much advantage after 6 ♗g2 against the 4...♕e7 variation, which is one of the safest lines for Black against 4 ♗d2. In the next chapter we consider the more active 6 ♘c3.

10 4 ♗d2 ♕e7 5 g3 ♘c6 6 ♘c3

After the sequence 1 d4 ♘f6 2 c4 e6 3 ♘f3 ♗b4+ 4 ♗d2 ♕e7 5 g3 ♘c6 White can also try 6 ♘c3. This move attempts to take advantage of the slightly awkward position of Black's knight on c6 and White hopes to gain the two bishops. Black usually opts for 6 ...♗xc3 or 6...d5 and we shall look at examples of each.

Game 73
Tatai-Ivkov
Albufiera 1978

1	d4	♘f6
2	c4	e6
3	♘f3	♗b4+
4	♗d2	♕e7
5	g3	♘c6
6	♘c3	

This move attempts to disrupt Black's development and take advantage of the position of Black's knight on c6. In many lines Black is obliged to surrender his king's bishop for the white knight on c3; here Black chooses to exchange voluntarily.

6	...	♗xc3
7	♗xc3	♘e4
8	♖c1	0-0

8...d6 is considered in the next game, Khalifman-Adams, and 8...d6 9 ♗g2 0-0 (or 8...0-0 9 ♗g2 d6) in Kramnik-Ulibin.

9	♗g2	a5
10	0-0	d6

Now White could play 11 d5 ♘b4 12 a3 and if 12...♘a2 13 ♗xg7 ♔xg7 14 ♖a1 regaining the piece or if 12...♘xc3 13 ♖xc3 ♘a6 14 dxe6 fxe6 with a slight advantage. White can also consider 11 ♘h4 f5?! (11...♘xc3 is probably better) 12 d5 ♘b4 13

♗e1 which was Rohde-Miles, San Francisco 1987. Tatai instead retains the dark-squared bishop.

11 ♗e1 f5

Again we have a Dutch pawn structure, though Black is not committed to a kingside attack.

12 d5 ♘d8

Not 12...cxd5 13 cxd5 when White has the open c-file.

13 ♘d2 ♘c5
14 ♘b3 b6

Black maintains his firm blockade on the queenside.

15 ♘xc5 bxc5
16 ♖c3

Instead 16 dxe6 ♖b8 17 ♕c2 ♘xe6 18 e3 ♗b7 19 ♗xa5 ♗xg2 20 ♔xg2 ♖a8 is fine for Black.

16 ... e5
17 f4 e4
18 ♖a3 ♘b7

Black has a weak pawn on a5, but as long as he can hold this White cannot make any progress on the queenside.

19 ♕c2 ♗d7
20 g4 c6
21 ♖g3 cxd5

22 cxd5 ♖ae8
23 gxf5 ♗xf5

White has switched to the kingside, but Black can defend.

24 ♗c3 ♖f7
25 ♔h1

Or 25 e3 c4 26 ♗d4 ♖c8 with the idea of ...♘c5-d3.

25 ... e3
26 ♖xg7+ ♖xg7
27 ♕xf5 ♖g6

White has sacrificed the exchange and has compensation in the form of the passed f-pawn.

28 ♕h5 ♘d8
29 f5 ♖g5

30	♕f3	♕f7
31	♕f4	♕h5
32	♗f3	♕h6
33	h4	♘f7

34	♔h2	♔f8
35	♔h3	♖g8
36	♕xh6+	♘xh6
37	♗h5	♖e4
38	f6	♘g4
39	f7	♘f2+
40	♖xf2	♖xh4+
	0-1	

After 41 ♔xh4 exf2 42 fxg8(♕) ♔xg8 White cannot stop the pawn from queening.

Black can also exchange on c3 and then play for ...e6-e5, which is one of his most reliable plans.

Game 74
Khalifman-Adams
Groningen 1990

1	d4	♘f6
2	c4	e6
3	♘f3	♗b4+
4	♗d2	♕e7
5	g3	♘c6
6	♘c3	♗xc3
7	♗xc3	♘e4
8	♖c1	d6
9	♗g2	♘xc3
10	♖xc3	e5
11	d5	♘b8
12	0-0	0-0
13	♘d2	

White has several alternatives here: 13 ♘e1 a5 14 e4 ♘a6; 13 ♕c2 a5; 13 e4 ♗g4 14 b4 a5 15 a3 ♘a6 and 13 b4 a5 14 ♖a3, all of which retain a slight advantage.

13	...	a5

14	c5

White breaks immediately on the queenside; 14 e4 ♘a6 15 f4 exf4 16 gxf4 f5 leads to equal play for Black, as in Piket-

Adams, Cannes 1992.

14	...	♘a6
15	cxd6	cxd6
16	♘c4	♛d8

17   a3

Now Black can push White back. 17 a4 is better even though White can make no further progress on the queenside; and also possible is 17 ♛b3 ♘c5 18 ♛b6.

17	...	b5
18	♘d2	♗d7
19	♛b1	b4
20	axb4	axb4
21	♖cc1	♘c5
22	♘e4	♗f5

The key to Black's plan; he will exchange off the white knight which will leave him with a superior minor piece.

23	♖c4	b3
24	♛c1	♗xe4
25	♗xe4	f5
26	♗g2	♛a5
27	h4	♛b5
28	♛c3	♘a4
29	♛b4	♛xb4
30	♖xb4	♖fb8
31	♖xb8+	♖xb8
32	♖b1	♖c8

White is unable to defend his b-pawn.

33	♗h3	g6
34	e4	♖c2
35	♖a1	♘c5
36	exf5	♖xb2
37	fxg6	hxg6
38	♗e6+	♚f8
39	♖a8+	♚e7
	0-1	

A fine positional game by Michael Adams.

Black must be careful not to allow White the advantage of the two bishops without obtaining active play in return, as the following game shows.

Game 75
Kramnik-Ulibin
Afitos-Nikitas 1992

1	d4	♘f6
2	c4	e6
3	♘f3	♗b4+
4	♗d2	♛e7
5	g3	♘c6
6	♘c3	0-0
7	♗g2	♗xc3
8	♗xc3	♘e4
9	♖c1	d6
10	d5	

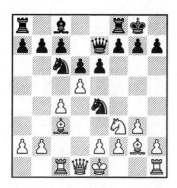

10   ...   ♘d8

Black has a more active alternative with 10...♘xc3 11 ♖xc3 ♘b8 12 ♘d4 (12 dxe6 fxe6 13 ♘d4 leads to a slightly better position for White) 12...e5 13 ♘c2 f5 14 0-0 ♘d7, as in Kouatly-Seirawan, Cannes 1992.

11   dxe6

The best move, by analogy with the previous note; 11 0-0 e5 12 ♕c2 f5 13 c5 ♘f7 gave Black an equal game in Eingorn-Miles, Zagreb (Interzonal) 1987.

11   ...   ♘xe6

The other recapture 11...fxe6

12 0-0 ♗d7 13 ♗e1 ♘f6 occurred in Korchnoi-Petrosian, Candidates match, Moscow 1971, when White was slightly better.

Now White is able to retain the two bishops.

12   ♗b4   ♗d7

Black could have tried to create play by either 12...♕f6 13 ♕c2 ♘6c5 14 0-0 ♗f5 (though after 15 ♘h4 White has the advantage since 15...♘xg3 16 fxg3 ♗xc2 17 ♖xf6 gxf6 18 ♖xc2 gives White a winning endgame) or 12...a5 13 ♗a3 ♘6g5 14 ♘xg5 ♘xg5 (though 15 c5 is awkward).

13   ♘e5   ♘6c5

13...♕f6 14 ♗xe4 ♕xe5 15 ♗xb7 ♕xb2 16 ♖b1 ♕xa2 17 ♗xa8 ♖xa8 18 ♕b3 ♕a6 gives Black some compensation for the exchange.

14	♘xd7	♘xd7
15	0-0	a5
16	♗a3	♖fe8

More energetic is 16...b6 with the idea of 17...♖ae8 and ...f7-f5.

17	b3	b6
18	♗b2	♖ad8
19	♕d4	♕f6
20	♕xf6	♘dxf6 (D)
21	♖fd1	h6
22	e3	♘d7
23	♔f1	♖e7
24	♔e2	♖de8
25	g4	♖e6
26	h4	♖6e7
27	♗f3	♘dc5
28	♖d5	♘a6
29	a3	♘ac5
30	b4	axb4
31	axb4	♘a6

32	b5	♘ac5
33	♖a1	♘f6
34	♖dd1	♘fe4
35	♖a7	♔f8

White now sacrifices a pawn to open the g- and h-files for his rooks.

36	g5	hxg5
37	hxg5	♘xg5
38	♗c6	♖c8
39	♖h1	♔g8
40	♖aa1	♘ce6
41	♖h4	f6
42	♖g1	♔f7
43	♗d5	♔e8
44	♖h8+	♘f8
45	f4	♘ge6
46	♔f3	f5
47	♖g6	♘c5
48	♗xg7	♖f7
49	♗xf8	1-0

Black's other option apart from exchanging on c3 is to counter in the centre with ...d7-d5, with positions similar to a Catalan or Queen's Gambit Declined.

Game 76
Kasparov-Garcia Gonzales
Moscow (Interzonal) 1982

1	d4	♘f6
2	c4	e6
3	♘f3	♗b4+
4	♗d2	♕e7
5	g3	♘c6
6	♘c3	d5

An unusual move which leads to a Queen's Gambit type of position in which Black's knight on c6 is not well placed. This is compensated by the difficulty for White in maintaining his pawn on c4 now that he is going to fianchetto his king's bishop. White decides to exchange on d5 but this frees Black's queen's bishop

7   cxd5

Also possible is 7 ♗g2, as in the game Piket-Korchnoi below.

7	...	exd5
8	♗g2	0-0

The less accurate 8...♗g4 is featured in the next game, Gligoric-Christiansen.

9	0-0	♖e8

Black has a number of playable alternatives here: 9...♗g4 10 a3 ♗xc3 11 ♗xc3 ♞e4 12 ♖c1 a5; 9...a5 10 ♕c2 ♗g4 11 e3 ♕d7; and 9...♖d8 10 a3 ♗xc3 11 ♗xc3 ♗f5. It is a matter of style which line the black player prefers.

10	♕b3

White obtained a slight advantage in Gligoric-A. Rodriguez, Lucerne (Olympiad) 1982, after 10 e3 ♗g4 11 ♕c2 ♕d7 12 ♖fc1 ♖e7 (perhaps 12...a5!? is better) 13 a3 ♗xc3 14 ♗xc3 ♞e4 15 b4.

10	...	♗g4
11	e3	a5! *(D)*

Black prepares to play ...a5-a4 which will lock up the queenside. White cannot capture on d5 as 12 ♞xd5 ♞xd5 13 ♕xd5 ♗xf3 followed by ...♗xd2 wins.

12	a3	♗xf3
13	♗xf3	a4
14	♕d1	♗xc3
15	♗xc3	♕d7

Now Black is planning to occupy the outpost on b3 by ...♞a5

and this forces White into further exchanges.

16	♖c1	♞a5
17	♗xa5	♖xa5
18	♖c5	♖ea8

18...♖xc5 is bad since it gives the white queen a good square on d4 after 19 dxc5.

19	♕c2	c6
20	♖c1	g6
21	♕d3	♔g7
22	♖1c3	h5
23	h4	♕e7
	½-½	

During the 1980s White had considerable success in this line because of the more dynamic nature of his position. A good example is the following game.

Game 77
Gligoric-Christiansen
Saint John 1988

1	d4	♞f6	4	♗d2	♕e7
2	c4	e6	5	g3	♞c6
3	♞f3	♗b4+	6	♞c3	d5

7	cxd5	exd5
8	♗g2	♗g4
9	0-0	

Not 9 e3? ♘xd4; but 9 ♗g5!? is worth consideration.

9	...	♗xf3
10	exf3	

White must not capture with the bishop: 10 ♗xf3 ♘xd4 11 ♘xd5 ♘xd5 (11...♘xf3+ 12 exf3 ♘xd5 13 ♖e1) 12 ♗xd5 0-0-0! with a very strong attack for Black.

10	...	0-0

If 10...♘xd4? 11 ♖e1 ♘e6 12 f4 and White has many threats.

11	♗g5!	♖ad8
12	f4!	♗xc3
13	bxc3	

White has the two bishops and play against d5 and b7 so Black has a difficult defensive task ahead.

13	...	h6
14	♖e1	

Also possible is 14 ♗h4 with the idea of f4-f5.

14	...	♕d6
15	♗h4!	♖d7

| 16 | f5 |

After 16 ♖e5 ♘e4!? Black has counterplay.

16	...	♖e7
17	♗xf6	

White could have retained the bishop pair with 17 ♖xe7!? ♘xe7 18 g4 also with good prospects.

17	...	♕xf6

Black could have held on to d5 with 17...♖xe1+ 18 ♕xe1 gxf6!? but this was unattractive.

18	♗xd5	♖xe1+
19	♕xe1	♕xf5
20	♗e4	♕d7

White's bishop is superior to the black knight and can attack on both sides of the board.

21	♕e2!	♖e8
22	♕f3	

Naturally White aims at b7.

22	...	g6

After 22...♘a5 23 ♗xb7 c5 24 ♗d5 cxd4 25 c4! White has strong play.

23	♖b1	♘a5
24	♗xb7	c6

24...♖b8 25 ♗e4 is good.

| 25 | ♗a6 | ♕e6 |

26	♗f1!	♕xa2
27	♕d1	♕a3
28	♕d2	h5
29	c4	♖d8
30	♕g5!?	♖e8
31	♕d2	♖d8
32	♕e1!	♘b3

Black must rescue his stranded knight against the threat of ♖a1. If 32...♖xd4 33 ♖b8+ ♔h7 34 ♕e5+ wins.

33	♕c3	♖b8
34	d5	a5

After 34...cxd5 35 cxd5 a5 36 d6 a4 37 ♕f6! ♕c5 38 ♖d1! wins.

35	dxc6	

Also good are 35 ♕f6 and 35 d6.

35	...	a4
36	♕f6	♕c5
37	♗g2	♕f5

Or 37...♕xc4 38 ♖d1.

38	♕xf5	gxf5
39	♖b2	♔f8
40	c5!	♔e7
41	♗d5	♖b5
42	♖e2+	♔d8
43	♗xf7	♖xc5
44	♖a2!	f4
45	♖xa4	f3
46	h4	♘c1
47	♖c4	♘e2+
48	♔h2	♖xc4
49	♗xc4	♔c7
50	♗f7	1-0

Black can defend solidly after ...d7-d5 with ...♖d8 and ...♗d7-e8. Although this is the best plan, and Korchnoi has shown that it is playable, it is not easy for Black to handle in practice.

Game 78
Piket-Korchnoi
Nijmegen 1993

1	d4	♘f6
2	c4	e6
3	♘f3	♗b4+
4	♗d2	♕e7
5	g3	♘c6
6	♘c3	d5
7	♗g2	0-0

A sharp alternative is 7...dxc4 8 0-0 0-0 9 ♗g5 h6 10 ♗xf6 ♕xf6 11 ♘e4 ♕e7 (11...♕f5 is another, possibly better, idea) 12 ♕c2 with a slight advantage for White, as in Hebden-King, London 1990.

8	a3	♗xc3

9		♗xc3

9	...	♘e4

10   ♖c1

Preferable is 10 ♕c2 as this is the natural square for the queen. The king's rook can then go to d1.

10	...	♖d8
11	♕c2	a5
12	0-0	♗d7
13	♖fe1	♗e8

Black has a solid position and may be able to re-deploy his bishop on f7, g6 or h5 after ...f7-f6 or ...f7-f5.

14   cxd5

This relaxation of the tension eases Black's task.

14	...	exd5
15	♘d2	f5
16	e3	♗g6
17	♕b3	♕d6
18	♘f3	a4
19	♕b5	♕d7
20	♘h4	♗f7
21	♗b4	♖a6

Black now has threats of ...♖b6.

22	f3	♘xb4
23	♕xd7	♖xd7
24	axb4	♘d6

25	♗h3	♗e6
26	e4	dxe4
27	d5	♗xd5
28	♘xf5	♘xf5
29	♗xf5	♗e6
30	b5	♖b6
31	♗xe6+	♖xe6
32	♖xe4	♖xe4
33	fxe4	

| 33 | ... | ♖d2 |
| 34 | ♖c4 | |

White cannot capture on c7 (34 ♖xc7 ♖xb2 35 ♖xb7 a3 36 ♖a7 a2 and Black wins) so he is forced to eliminate Black's dangerous a-pawn.

34	...	♖xb2
35	♖xa4	♖xb5
36	♖d4	♔f8
37	♖d7	♖c5
38	♔f2	♖c3
39	e5	b5
40	e6	b4
41	♖f7+	♔e8
42	♖xg7	b3
43	♔e2	♖c6
44	♔d3	b2
45	♖g8+	♔e7
46	♖b8	♖b6

47	♖xb6	cxb6
48	♔c2	♔xe6
	0-1	

6 ♘c3 is a strong line against

which Black must fight hard to equalize. The most reliable choice is to exchange on c3, follow up with ...♘e4xc3 and then play ...e6-e5.

11 Keres Defence

Black can also try a kind of accelerated Bogo-Indian, known as the Keres Defence, with 1 d4 e6 2 c4 ♗b4+. This move has independent significance and was played by Réti against Vidmar at Mannheim 1914. Subsequently it was adopted by the Estonian grandmaster Paul Keres in the late 1930s with success and remains a popular choice.

After 2...♗b4+ White has three sensible choices: he can reply with 3 ♘c3 when Black has several options - 3...♘f6 (transposing to the Nimzo-Indian Defence), 3...c5, 3...f5 (with a Dutch formation) or 3...b6; he can play 3 ♗d2 when Black again has several options - 3...a5, 3...c5 or 3...♕e7; or interpose 3 ♘d2 when Black again has a choice but most popular has been 3 ...c5. Because of the flexibility of choice for Black, 2...♗b4+ is one of the most fertile areas of development in the Bogo-Indian complex.

Game 79
Alekhine-Keres
Bad Nauheim 1936

1	d4	e6
2	c4	♗b4+
3	♘c3 *(D)*	
3	...	c5

Black can also play the more adventurous 3...b6, transposing to the English Defence, as in Zsu. Polgar-Speelman Volmac 1993, which continued 4 e4 ♗b7 5 d5 ♕e7 6 ♗e2 ♘f6 7 f3 exd5 8 cxd5 c6 9 dxc6 ♘xc6 10 ♘h3 d5! 11 exd5 0-0-0 12 ♗g5 ♖he8 13 ♗xf6 gxf6! 14 ♘f4 ♕e5 15 ♕d2

♗xc3! 16 bxc3 ♘b4 17 ♔f2? ♘xd5 18 ♘d3 ♘xc3! 0-1.

4 dxc5

Capablanca-Keres, AVRO 1938, transposed to a Nimzo-Indian with 4 e3 ♘f6 5 ♘ge2 cxd4 6 exd4 0-0 7 a3 ♗e7 8 ♘f4 d5 9 cxd5 ♘xd5 10 ♘fxd5 exd5 11 ♕b3 ♘c6 12 ♗e3 ♗f6 13 ♖d1 ♗g4 14 ♗e2 ♗xe2 15 ♔xe2 ♖e8 with equality, but Alekhine typically takes up the challenge.

4 ... ♗xc3+
5 bxc3

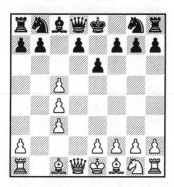

White's two bishops compensate for his shattered pawn structure.

5 ... ♕a5
6 ♘f3 ♘f6

If 6...♕xc3+ 7 ♗d2 ♕xc4 8 ♖c1 and White has good compensation for the sacrificed pawn.

7 e3 0-0
8 ♘d4 ♘e4

Black must take on c5 before White can play ♘b3.

9 ♗b2 ♘xc5
10 ♘b3 ♕c7
11 ♘xc5 ♕xc5

12 ♕b3

This move underlines White's lead in development and leaves Black in difficulties.

12 ... d6
13 ♖d1 ♖d8
14 ♗a3 ♕e5
15 c5 d5
16 c4 ♘c6
17 ♗e2 dxc4
18 ♖xd8+ ♘xd8
19 ♕xc4 ♕d5

Black offers the exchange of queens to ease his position; 19...♕a1+ 20 ♗d1 only helps White.

20 ♕xd5 exd5

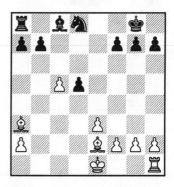

White has the advantage in the endgame because of the bishop pair.

21 ♔d2 ♗d7
22 ♖b1 ♗c6
23 ♔c3 ♖c8
24 ♔b4 f6
25 ♗g4 ♖c7
26 ♖d1 ♖e7
27 ♗f3 ♖d7
28 ♗b2 ♔f7
29 h4 ♘e6

30	♗e2	♖d8
31	♗d4	♖c8

Black is reluctant to exchange on d4 as this would leave the d-pawn more exposed.

32	a4	♔e7
33	♗b5	♗e8
34	♖c1	b6

A fine tactical resource. White cannot advance the c-pawn because of its capture after 35 c6 ♔d6, and Black threatens to win the c-pawn with ...a7-a5+.

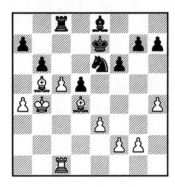

35	cxb6	♖xc1

36	b7	♘d8
37	b8(♕)	♘c6+
38	♗xc6	♖b1+
39	♔a5	♖xb8
40	♗xd5	♔d6

Black still has a difficult task to draw the endgame because of White's bishops.

41	♗c4	♔c7
42	g4	♗c6
43	g5	♔b7
44	f4	fxg5
45	hxg5	♖e8
46	f5	♗e4
47	♗e6	♖f8
48	♗xg7	♖xf5+
49	♗xf5	♗xf5
50	♔b5	♗d3+
51	♔c5	♔c7
52	♔d5	♔d7
53	♗d4	a6
54	♗c5	a5
55	♔e5	♗c2
	½-½	

Black can also opt for a Dutch formation after 3 ♘c3 with 3...f5.

Game 80
Suba-Speelman
British Championship, Plymouth 1990

1	d4	e6
2	c4	♗b4+
3	♘c3	f5 *(D)*
4	♗d2	

Landau-Alekhine, Kemeri 1937, went instead 4 ♕b3 ♕e7 5 a3 ♗xc3+ 6 ♕xc3 ♘f6 7 ♘f3 ♘c6 8 b4 b6 9 ♗b2 ♗b7 10 g3 ♘e4 11 ♕b3 a5 12 b5 a4 13 ♕c2 ♘a5 14 ♗g2 ♘d6 15 c5 ♘dc4 16 cxb6 cxb6 17 0-0 ♖c8 18 ♗c3 ♘b3 19 ♗b4 d6 20 ♖ac1 0-0 21 ♕a2 ♘xc1 22 ♖xc1 ♘e5 23 ♖xc8 ♘xf3+ 24 ♗xf3 ♖xc8 25 ♗xb7 ♖c1+ 26 ♔g2 ♕xb7+ 27 f3 ♕d5 28 ♕xd5 exd5 29 ♗xd6 ♖b1 30

♔f2 ♖xb5 31 ♔e3 ♖b2 32 ♔d3
♔f7 33 h4 g6 0-1.

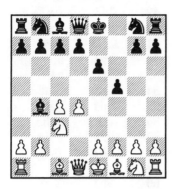

4	...	♘f6
5	e3	0-0
6	♗d3	d6
7	♕c2	♘c6
8	♘ge2	♕d7

Black transfers the queen to f7
this way rather than via e8,
avoiding ♘b5.

9	f3	e5
10	0-0	♕f7
11	a3	♗xc3
12	♗xc3	♗d7
13	c5	

White must not capture on f5:
13 ♗xf5 ♗xf5 14 ♕xf5 ♕xc4
with advantage to Black because
of the threat against e2.

13	...	♘d5
14	♗d2	exd4
15	♘xd4	♘xd4
16	exd4	♕f6
17	♔h1	♔h8

Black avoids the risky 17...
♕xd4 which opens the game for
White's bishops and rooks.

| 18 | ♖ad1 | ♗e6 |
| 19 | ♖fe1 | ♗g8 |

| 20 | cxd6 | cxd6 |

Black has a well posted knight
on d5 but must be careful not to
allow White's bishop pair into the
game.

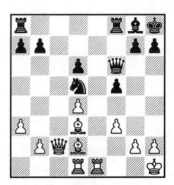

21	♕a4	a6
22	♗b1	b5
23	♕a5	♕h4
24	♗c1	g5
25	♖e2	♖f6
26	♕e1	♕h5
27	♔g1	♖af8

White is now able to win the
exchange at the cost of a weakened kingside.

28	♗xf5	♖xf5
29	g4	♕h3
30	gxf5	♕xf3
31	♖f2	♕h3
32	♕f1	♕h5
33	♖d3	♘f4
34	♗xf4	gxf4 *(D)*

The threat of ...♗c4 forces
White to unpin his queen, so he
does not have time to capture on
f4. This allows Black to capture
on f5 and leaves White in trouble.

| 35 | ♕h3 | ♕g5+ |
| 36 | ♕g2 | ♕xf5 |

The New Bogo-Indian

37	♕h3	♕g6+
38	♖g3	♕b1+
39	♕f1	♕e4
40	♖gf3	♗d5

Black's bishop dominates the position.

41	h3	♕xd4
42	♕d3	♖g8+
43	♔h2	♕g7
44	♕c3	♗xf3
45	♖xf3	♕xc3

46	♖xc3	♔g7
47	♖d3	♔f7
48	♖xd6	f3
49	♖d3	♖g2+
50	♔h1	♖xb2
51	♖xf3+	♔e6
52	♔g1	a5
53	♔f1	a4
54	♔e1	♔d5
55	♔d1	♖b3
56	♖xb3	axb3
57	♔c1	♔d4
58	♔b2	♔c4
59	h4	h5
60	♔b1	♔c3
61	♔c1	b2+
62	♔b1	♔b3
63	a4	♔xa4
	0-1	

If White counters with 3 ♗d2 then Black can reply with 3...c5, 3...♕e7 (well met here by 4 e4!) or 3...a5 as in the following game.

Game 81
Benjamin-Eingorn
Reykjavik (Summit) 1990

1	d4	e6
2	c4	♗b4+
3	♗d2	a5
4	g3	d6
5	♘f3	♘c6
6	♘c3	

A good alternative for White is 6 ♗g2 e5 7 d5 ♗xd2+ 8 ♕xd2 ♘b8 9 0-0 ♘h6 10 ♘e1 0-0 11 ♘d3 when he is well placed for developments on either side of the board, as in Oll-Ward,

Copenhagen 1993.

6	...	♘f6
7	♗g2	e5
8	d5	♘e7
9	0-0	0-0
10	♘e1	♗c5
11	♔h1	♗a7

A most unusual position to arise from the Bogo-Indian, with the black bishop retreating to a7. The bishop would be well placed here if White were to play e2-e4, so White opts to play e2-e3.

12	♘d3	♘d7
13	e3	f5
14	f4	e4

This blocks off the white bishop on g2.

15	♘f2	♘f6
16	h3	♕e8
17	♖g1	♗d7
18	♗f1	c6

Black undermines the white pawn centre which leaves his minor pieces with more space.

19	dxc6	♗xc6
20	♖c1	♔h8
21	♗g2	d5
22	c5	♘d7
23	♘a4	♗xa4
24	♕xa4	♘xc5
25	♕xa5	♘e6
26	♕b4	d4
27	♕b3	dxe3
28	♗xe3	♗xe3
29	♕xe3	

Black now has a clear advantage because of the poor state of White's bishop on g2 and knight on f2.

| 29 | ... | ♕b5 |

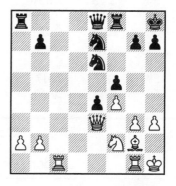

Not 29...♖xa2 30 ♕b3 winning. Now White loses a pawn.

30	♗f1	♕xb2
31	♗c4	♕d4
32	♘d1	♕xe3
33	♘xe3	♘d4
34	♖gd1	♖fd8
35	♖b1	♖ab8
36	♖b6	g6
37	♔g2	♘ec6
38	♔f2	♖d7
39	♗e6	♖e7
40	♗d5	♖a8
41	♖db1	♖a7
42	g4	♖d7
43	♖1b2	♔g7
44	gxf5	gxf5
45	♖d2	♔f8
46	♗e6	♖g7
47	♗d5	♖a3
48	♖db2	♘e7
49	♗xb7	♘g6

White is forced to give up the exchange to avoid the loss of the f-pawn.

50	♖xg6	hxg6
51	h4	♘e6
52	♘g2	♘c5
53	♖b5	♖xa2+

54	♔g3	♖a3+
55	♔h2	♘d3
56	♖b6	♘f2
57	♔g1	♘g4
58	♖b1	♔e8
59	♔f1	♔d7
60	♖b4	♔c7

61	♘e1	♖a2
62	♔g1	♘f6
	0-1	

3 ♘d2 is more combative than 3 ♗d2, but again Black has sufficient resources.

Game 82
Lev-Eingorn
London (Lloyds Bank) 1989

1	d4	e6
2	c4	♗b4+
3	♘d2	c5

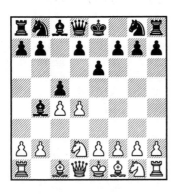

4	a3	♗xd2+
5	♕xd2	cxd4
6	♘f3	♘f6
7	♘xd4	

I. Sokolov-Dorfman, Burgas 1992, went instead 7 ♕xd4!? ♘c6 8 ♕d1 0-0 9 e3 e5! 10 b4 d6 11 ♗e2 a5 12 b5 ♘e7 with good play for Black.

7	...	0-0
8	g3	

This leaves the white pawn on c4 without protection. In Gulko-

Romero Holmes, Leon 1992, White preferred 8 e3 d5 9 b4 a5?! (9...b6!?) 10 b5 with good play for White.

8	...	d5

9	cxd5	♕xd5
10	♘f3	♕b5
11	a4	♕h5
12	♗g2	

12 ♕g5 is worth consideration, exchanging queens.

12	...	♘c6
13	0-0	h6
14	b4	♖d8
15	♕e1	e5
16	b5	♘d4

17	♘xd4	exd4
18	♗f4	♘d5
19	♕d2	♘xf4
20	♕xf4	♕xe2

22	♕c7	♕d7
23	♕xd7	♗xd7
24	♗xb7	♖ab8
25	♗c6	♗e6
26	♖ed1	d3
27	♖d2	♗c4
28	♖c1	♖d4
29	f3	♗b3
30	♖c3	♗xa4
31	♖cxd3	♖xd3
32	♖xd3	a6
33	♖c3	axb5
34	♖d3	♗c2
35	♖d2	♗b3
36	♔f2	b4
37	♖b2	♗e6
38	♔e3	0-1

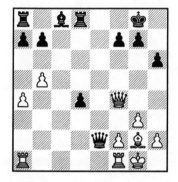

Although Black has won a pawn, White still has considerable pressure against b7 and Black is forced to return the pawn to develop his queen's bishop.

21	♖fe1	♕g4

2...♗b4+ gives Black many transpositional possibilities and remains an area of the Bogo-Indian where there is plenty of scope for innovation.

Index of Complete Games